The Second Year of

THE

Nixon Watch

The Second Year of
THE
Nixon Watch

BY

JOHN OSBORNE

Illustrated by BILL MAULDIN

Introduction by DAVID BRODER

LIVERIGHT

NEW YORK

LIVERIGHT

This book consists of articles that appeared in *The New Republic* between January 1970 and January 1971. The title is derived from "'The Nixon Watch,'" the standing head under which John Osborne reports the Presidency for that magazine. Apart from some changes of tense for present clarity, the correction of typographical and similar errors, and the addition of updating addenda at the end of a few chapters, the originals have not been altered for this publication. All articles are reprinted by permission of the publisher.

Standard Book Number: 87140–517–2
Library of Congress Catalog Card Number: 74–150589
Printed in the United States of America

CONTENTS

INTRODUCTION

BY DAVID BRODER

There was a fine symmetry to the ceremonies by which Mr. Nixon opened and closed his second year as President. On New Year's Day, 1970, he signed the Environmental Protection Act, with a noble pledge to see that "America pays its debts to the past by reclaiming the purity of its air, its water, and our living environment."

On Dec. 31, 1970, he signed the most notable environmental measure of the year—the Clean Air Act—in another White House ceremony, but this one was marred by a political maneuver of almost stupefying cheapness. The chief congressional sponsor of the legislation, Senator Edmund S. Muskie of Maine, who also happened to be the leading prospect for the 1972 Democratic presidential nomination, was omitted from the list of those invited to witness the signing. And the headlines dwelled, not on the President's redeeming a major pledge, but on his administering a minor snub to a seemingly much-feared rival.

The shrinkage of large hopes to small (and often mean-spirited) gestures characterized too much of Mr. Nixon's 1970. The second year was not a notable one for the President. With his fondness for the idiom of sports, Mr. Nixon himself might suggest he was fighting a "Sophomore jinx" after burning up the league in his rookie year as President in 1969. (Can anyone think now of Richard Nixon as a rookie anything? Perhaps not.)

The second year began with Mr. Nixon leading the league in all departments. He had reaped a world of praise for the success of the

first manned landings on the moon. He had established himself as
the President, in fact as well as in name, by impressing the leaders
of Europe and Asia on his first overseas trips and by demonstrating
to his domestic constituents in a series of effective speeches and
press conferences a confidence and command of events many of
them were surprised to find in him.

He had put in motion a policy designed to redeem his most important campaign pledge—ending the war in Vietnam—and he had
received the first visible dividend from that policy, with the return
to America from the battle zone of the first large contingents of
US forces.

In October and November, 1969, he had withstood—and, indeed, routed—the strongest organized challenge to that policy by
rallying public opinion to condemn the mass protest marches organized by students and politicians demanding immediate withdrawal.

Democrats glumly conceded that Mr. Nixon had seized the high
ground on the main foreign policy issue, and they worried that he
was going to preempt the same advantage by his domestic efforts
to contain inflation and crime. Republican candidates allied with
Mr. Nixon won the only two governorships up for election in 1969,
taking the important states of Virginia and New Jersey from the
opposition. The Democrats were $9 million in debt; their leadership
was in disarray, and, as they acknowledged in candid moments
themselves, they did not have much to propose that Mr. Nixon was
not already doing.

In that New Year's Day statement on the Environmental Protection Act, Mr. Nixon put in a strong bid for personal proprietorship
of what some were calling "the issue of the decade." Three weeks
later, in his State of the Union message, he reached back for a
phrase he had used in the first speech of his campaign for the presidency, and summoned Americans to experience "the lift of a driving
dream which has made America from its beginning the hope of the
world."

It was all very heady, but the year that began so buoyantly ended
with Mr. Nixon rather frantically reshuffling his Cabinet, his
Administration, and his party leadership. As he prepared to meet
a revived Democratic Party opposition, strengthened in Congress
and the state capitols by the mid-term election, he confronted a
massive budget deficit, high unemployment, and high prices. The

1972 election campaign suddenly seemed to be very difficult indeed.

The triumphs of the second year were of the synthetic variety—from the Apollo 13 mission, which returned its crew to earth without landing on the moon, to the bold raid on the prisoner of war camp outside Hanoi, which cost no American lives but, tragically, found no prisoners, either.

The Middle East peace initiative and the President's Mediterranean journey were thrown off stride by the untimely death of Nasser. The great welfare reform effort died in snarling misunderstanding between the White House and its natural allies on Capitol Hill. The mid-term election offensive, designed to break the Democrats' grip on the Senate, was blocked by the sagging economy and perhaps by the excesses of the President's and Vice President's rhetoric.

And along the way there were the Carswell nomination, Cambodia, Kent State, Jackson State, the Scranton Report, and the steady crescendo of statistics measuring the rapid increase of both prices and unemployment. By the end of the year, there was growing suspicion among many of Mr. Nixon's fellow-Republicans, his well-wishers, and those who yearned for some glimmer of hope of progress against America's manifold problems that the situation was somehow slipping out of his control—that events were ordering him, not the other way around.

I watched Mr. Nixon's second year from an unusual perspective. After fifteen unbroken years as a reporter in Washington, I took a sabbatical at Harvard University's Institute of Politics that took me out of day-to-day contact with the White House and Capitol Hill and let me see the President in the way most of his fellow-citizens do: through television and the newspapers. True, in the academic-political community of Cambridge, he was much more at the center of our thoughts than he is in most American communities. His actions, statements, strategies, and motivations were the grist for daily analysis at lunch and tea and dinner. But these were still outsiders' discussions; none of us had intimate access to the White House circle, or, if we did, we were not exploiting it.

When I returned to my job at *The Washington Post* in the fall of 1970, I was plunged immediately into coverage of the mid-term campaign, and was immersed in the voters' reaction to Mr. Nixon as President and campaigner.

Throughout the year, then, I was seeing him as he appeared to outsiders—and to myself, as a journalistic outsider, as well. Only now, as this is written, in the final months of 1970, have I had the opportunity to compare my impressions with those of men who have worked intimately with Mr. Nixon and who cover him day by day.

One man's attitude was particularly striking—a Nixon admirer who had left the White House staff during the President's second year to resume his legal career. We were talking of the turmoil inside the Administration following the Cambodian invasion and the wave of campus protests. As the discussion went on, and he thought back to those days, he became more and more agitated, pounding his fist into his palm, and finally he burst out, almost in a sob, "Dammit, it didn't have to be this way. It didn't have to be."

I believe he was right: ". . . it didn't have to be this way." But if the change—the deterioration—in the quality of the Nixon Administration's performance in its second year was not inevitable, neither was it accidental. It stemmed, rather, from the President's personality, from the character of the men with whom he surrounded himself, and from the nature of the modern presidency.

To take these matters in reverse order, it may well be that there is a process that works in all Administrations to restrict the President's horizons of perception. Characteristically, a new President enters office with two pictures in his mind. One is the picture of the country he has seen during his campaign, a country (as he will have described it in his speeches) beset by problems but not devoid of hope, ready to respond to leadership. The second picture is of that ideal country (and ideal world) he has sketched as his goal in the speeches that earned him the presidency.

His primary concern upon taking office is to close the gap between that real world and the idealized world. He outlines his policies in his first year and—shock, disillusionment—finds many of them greeted by skepticism, indifference, or outright opposition.

At this point, two things happen. The President persists in his policies but, privately or publicly, he condemns his critics to perdition, dismisses them as blind men or worse, and instinctively recategorizes the world into "those who are with us and those who are not."

Second, his perceptions change. The longer he is in office; the less "real" becomes the real world, with its problems and dangers, and the more "real" becomes his idealized world—the world to which he is leading us.

At the end of Mr. Nixon's second year, the White House issued a summary of his "accomplishments" which seemed absurd—until one realized that, to the men involved, the act of proposing legislation, or announcing a policy, somehow conveys the sensation that the goals the legislation or policy seek have been accomplished. Symbol becomes substance.

There is another, closely related change that occurs in all Administrations—the substitution of process for product. In those same year-end briefings, officials could stand up and claim that great improvements had been made in the internal operations of the presidential office, disregarding the fact that—as Mr. Osborne demonstrates in several of his essays—the Nixon Administration has been plagued so often by almost incomprehensible blunders that a serious question has been raised about the competence of its most critical operations.

There was hardly a Cabinet officer, Republican Senator, or Governor by the end of the second year who did not have his own catalog of horror stories about his efforts to deal with—or get a response from—the White House bureaucracy. But the men involved were fascinated by the machinery they had created—and believed it to be working beautifully.

This preoccupation with the technology of management reflects something, also, of the personality of Richard Nixon. A particularly manipulative politician, he has turned out to take a particularly managerial approach to the office of President. Mr. Nixon, the candidate we all came to know over the years, had some rather remarkable talents. He could deliver anything from a thirty-second spot commercial to a thirty-minute speech "to time," without rehearsal or outside prompting, responding simply to an internal clock. He could go into a dozen congressional districts in three days and never fluff or hesitate on the name and accomplishments of the local candidate. He knew more about—and was more adept at—the mechanics of politics than anyone I ever knew.

What escaped him, most of the time, was the instinctive gesture or response, and also the larger vision—the theme—that gave a coherence to his tactics.

In 1968, however, he seemed to have discovered that theme—
the longing of a traumatized nation to be made whole again. In
the major addresses of his first year in office, he returned time and
again to the central concerns of the nation that had elected him,
urging and acting to reduce the scale of the war, to calm domestic
tempers, to restore balance to the economy.

But the longer he was in office, the harder Mr. Nixon seemed
to find it to relate tactics to strategy: which is to say, the harder
he found it to remember his major themes. My guess is that he is
not an instinctive enough politician to "feel" where the people are.
He learns the hard way—by exposure—and the modern presidency,
as George Reedy has pointed out, makes exposure difficult for a
President, rather than facilitating it.

Contributing to this difficulty has been the kind of staff Mr.
Nixon has chosen. Except for Henry Kissinger and the departed
Daniel Patrick Moynihan, it is largely a staff of campaign "func-
tionaries" (to borrow Spiro Agnew's word for Rogers C. B. Morton), men who were much more involved with schedules, schemes,
and techniques than with ideas or goals or strategies.

Their record in 1970 offered strong evidence not only that this
arrangement is inadequate for the presidency but that it is positively
damaging for an effective presidency.

It was the small-mindedness of the White House that produced
decisions like the exclusion of Muskie from the Clean Air Bill-
signing ceremony, or the naïve idea that the best use of a President
in a mid-term campaign was to send him around the country imply-
ing that the opposition party was "soft" on radicals, bomb-throwers,
or criminals. It was small-mindedness that kept the President from
apologizing for four months for his slip of the tongue in character-
izing Charles Manson as being guilty of the murders for which he
was then standing trial. It was small-mindedness that caused him to
treat the rejection of the unfortunate Mr. Carswell as evidence of
anti-South bias in the Senate.

It was a form of small-mindedness—the predominance of tactic
over strategy—that caused him to approve the Cambodian raid
and to be surprised by the reaction to it. It was a small-minded
conception of the presidency that made him so reluctant to invoke
the prestige of that office to curb the unconscionable wage and
price hikes of his first two years.

This is my view, and I think there is support for it in the incidents that Mr. Osborne describes in this book. But it is not a view that is limited to liberal journalists.

I think this is what Pat Moynihan was driving at, when he urged in his farewell to the Cabinet and the White House staff, at the end of 1970, that they should be "far more attentive" to what the President had said and proposed, because his "initial thrusts" were not being "followed up with a sustained, reasoned, reliable second and third order of advocacy." What Moynihan conveyed was an insider's sense that the strategic impulses, the occasional insights, of Mr. Nixon's presidency were being smothered, not encouraged, by the Administration he had constructed—which is, I think, an accurate judgment. Small-mindedness is incompatible with large enterprises, and the presidency is a place for large enterprises.

Even Kevin P. Phillips, John Mitchell's favorite political thinker, observed at the end of the Administration's second year that "President Nixon . . . faces a growing crisis of confidence in his leadership" because "Mr. Nixon, surrounded by a coterie of managerial-type pragmatists, has changed policies and directions so often —and sometimes so erratically—that the image is one of opportunism rather than vision. And so long as he continues to surround himself with managerial 'problem-solvers,' rather than framework-builders, he will not be able to change this uninspiring image. . . ."

That states the proposition very well, I believe, and leaves the matter where it properly belongs—in the President's hands. The second year of the Nixon Administration was one of steady deterioration in the quality of performance and leadership. Reversing that process is Mr. Nixon's largest challenge—and a political imperative for his survival in 1972.

The Second Year of
T H E
Nixon Watch

I

Henry's Wonderful Machine

During an inquiry in January of 1970 into the evolution and work-ings of the policy process devised and operated for President Nixon by his assistant for national security affairs, Henry A. Kissinger, several people who are involved in the process at the White House and in the State Department were asked whether they could think of any major decisions or departures in foreign policy that would not have occurred if the Kissinger system—"Henry's wonderful machine," I had come to call it—did not exist.

One of Kissinger's principal assistants answered: "No. But I do think the decisions have been better defined and conceived, their consequences have been better estimated and projected, than they would have been without it." Another said: "There probably has been no decision made or policy adopted that wouldn't have been if this system did not exist, but there's a much keener awareness of what we are doing, a better understanding of the consequences." A State Department man who works closely with both Kissinger and

Secretary of State William P. Rogers answered: "That's very hard to say. I don't think you can really answer that question." A deputy assistant secretary who is much occupied with meeting the Kissinger staff's demands upon the department said: "No, I shouldn't think so. It may have resulted in a few cases in our being better prepared to deal with problems that may arise—in the sense of identifying the courses that may be taken and of estimating the consequences in advance." Another deputy assistant secretary who is similarly occupied said: "How effective it all has been is a little hard to say. It has got the interested agencies involved, it has influenced the higher levels, but the extent to which it has actually affected policy is a subject that requires further study." Didn't he get some measure of the impact by comparing ultimate decisions with the papers that the interagency group with which he works submitted to the President through the Kissinger machine? "Once in a while you do," he replied. "I've seen a couple of instances of cause-and-effect, but it's been less than one would expect."

As all of the quoted officials pointed out, in one way and another, my question and their answers could produce an unfair and, to policy professionals, an irrelevant judgment of the process and its worth to Mr. Nixon. Its purpose, they argued, is not to determine policy or even necessarily to affect policy decisions. The purpose is to inform the makers of policy—officialdom would say, *the* maker of policy, the President—so thoroughly and so well that the final decision is at least based upon the best attainable understanding of all that is involved and the best attainable estimate of the probable consequences. That is what the Kissinger system is designed to accomplish. A judgment as to whether it does or not would require a knowledge of the information, of the nature and range of the choices provided the President through the process, that is denied the outside inquirer. One can only examine the process itself, and marvel that so many people go to so much trouble for so little demonstrable result.

The preparations for the Strategic Arms Limitation Talks (SALT) with the Soviet Union in the preliminary phase recently concluded at Helsinki and in the substantive phase soon to begin in Vienna have by all accounts been the most thorough of their kind, and they have been and still are being made within the Kissinger system. But the actual positions to be taken are still under review; the President has yet to make the decisive choices by which he and the process that informs his choices will be judged. Three meetings of the National Security Council, the Cabinet-level group at the apex of the system, and countless man-hours of NSC staff study and calculation went into the Middle East policy outlined in early 1970 by Secretary Rogers. But its essentials—the Israelis should withdraw from most of the Arab territory seized by them in 1967, the Arabs must accept the fact of Israel and come to peaceful terms with it—were implicit in Nixon statements before he was elected and were outlined to the Senate Foreign Relations Committee by Rogers on March 27, 1969, long before the NSC and departmental studies then under way were completed. A basic "China paper" was cleared through the Kissinger system in 1969. But Nixon had set forth the essentials of his present approach to China and to American commitments in Asia—he wants negotiation with Peking, he proposes to sustain all of the commitments at reduced and minimal cost to the United States—in a *Foreign Affairs* article published in October 1967. The interdepartmental group (IG) that deals with Far Eastern policy for Kissinger at the agency level had nothing to do with the specific decisions to relax restrictions upon travel and trade with Communist China. An American invitation to Peking to renew ambassadorial talks in Warsaw after a two-year lapse was issued by Rogers in February 1969, when the Kissinger system barely existed. The Nixon policy of gradual disengagement from Vietnam, meanwhile urging and awaiting substantive negotiation with Hanoi and the NLF in Paris, has been and still is the subject of intensive NSC and departmental labor, but I find it interesting that in 10 days of inquiry not one policy official attributed it to the Kissinger process as such.

At the peak and center of the Kissinger process is his own White House staff—formally, The National Security Council staff. It keeps growing (from 27 functional officers at the start last year to 44 listed on a roster dated January 8) and most of the growth is in the two administrative sections that serve Kissinger himself. His personal staff, headed by Brigadier General Alexander Haig, an Army man, has doubled (from three to six). The staff secretariat has seven people doing what two tried to do earlier. There are 19 "operators," five "planners" (two of whom double as "operators"), and eight "program analysts." Trying to define and differentiate their functions is a stupefying exercise, partly for the excellent reason that the operators plan, the planners operate, and the analysts do some of both. All of them contribute to the objective described by Kissinger in the spring of 1968, when he was advising Governor Rockefeller on foreign policy and didn't dream that he would be Mr. Nixon's chief staff adviser on that subject, in remarks to a University of California (Los Angeles) seminar. He said that a new President who wants to change the direction and mechanics of policy "must do so within the first four months. He need not complete it within this time, but he must give enough of a shake to the bureaucracy to indicate that he wants a new direction and he must be brutal enough to demonstrate that he means it."

Kissinger has served Nixon as, among other things, his surrogate brutalitarian. Whether the President has really given foreign policy as a whole "a new direction" is questionable. But there can be no question that the brutality has had much if not all of the desired effect upon its principal target, the bureaucracy of the Department of State. A humbler and more quiescent lot of departmental officials is not to be found in Washington. This is partly, if paradoxically, because they have acquired a heartening sense of confidence in their Secretary, William Rogers, who after months of seeming indifference to the woes and problems of the department has begun to assert his right of command over it, along with his prerogatives as the President's senior constitutional adviser on foreign policy. Given their recent assurance that somebody really is up there on the secretarial Seventh Floor, looking after them and at last countering Henry Kissinger's preeminence in the public mind, they came to accept as a fact of governmental life intrusions and demands from the Kissinger apparatus that had seemed to be intolerable. Department officers who all but hissed when they said "Kissinger" now speak of "Henry" in the tone of intimacy that is heard when members of his own staff talk about him. The department bureaucracy has recognized the fact that "Henry" is indeed a surrogate, speaking and acting for the President along lines and through organizational channels that Nixon conceived for himself and authorized Kissinger to implement in structural detail. "This is the way the President wants it," State's people tell each other. The nature of officialdom being what it is, what a President is known to want is more acceptable than anything a mere staff subordinate, however eminent, is supposed to want.

Organization and method apart, the atmosphere encountered after a year among Kissinger's assistants in the White House basement and across the street in the Executive Office Building encourages a belief that "Henry's machine" justifies all the pain and effort that have accompanied its establishment and evolution. The rather negative appraisals quoted at the beginning of this report reflect a modesty of claim that is refreshing in itself. It is good to hear one of Henry's planners say of a particular study project: "Our whole posture in Laos is subject to critical disagreement. Outsiders ask searching questions about it, so why shouldn't insiders ask them?" And of the President's vaunted "new direction" in Europe: "We have a stance, an attitude, in Europe that is well defined. But it isn't a policy. It doesn't add up 'by itself' in a coordinated way, to a policy that takes into account all of the issues and factors that ought to be considered together." Or to hear a Kissinger operator, one of the geographic officers charged with oversight of departmental activity in his area, say of the Middle East (which is not his responsibility but does concern him): "We have a fairly coherent policy and strategy for that area. But it's always subject to reassessment. What do you find if you project the present policy forward four or five years? Will it make a difference if you do? We ask the question, and try to suggest the best answers we can."

Kissinger's continuing dissatisfaction with many of the answers —the famous options demanded by Nixon and submitted to him through Henry, principally from State—is a subject of interesting comment among his subordinates. Some of them believe that he is unduly harsh, that the quality of many of the incoming policy papers has been quite high, and they imply that some of the NSC staff work devoted to analyzing, criticizing, and supplementing the departmental papers is wasted. Wasted, that is, unless Henry's needs are considered. Constantly driven and consulted by Nixon, and subject to a multitude of other demands upon his time, Kissinger is compelled to draw down his own "intellectual capital" and looks to his assistants and to the departmental staffs at their beck, to replenish it. A thinker by profession, deprived of adequate time for thought, he is said to expect "not a substitute for his own thinking, but a sort of analytical supplement to his thinking." Nixon considers himself to be a thinker. The quoted remark about Henry Kis-

singer may be a good definition of the principal service that he tries
to render the President.

January 31, 1970

———

On January 16, 1971, in a letter to Kissinger, the President thanked
him for deciding to remain at the White House awhile longer instead of returning to Harvard, and said: "Frankly, I cannot imagine
what the government would be like without you." Max Frankel of
the *New York Times,* concluding an exhaustive examination of the
foreign-policy process by other members of that newspaper's staff,
noted on January 24, 1971, that "even a lengthy study of how Mr.
Nixon has organized the management of international affairs leaves
the question of what difference it all makes to the substance of his
politics."

A Look
at John Mitchell

At the beginning of an interview with Attorney General John N.
Mitchell, I said that I'd like to hear from him an accurate statement
of his relationship with and influence upon President Nixon. Mr.
Mitchell settled into his chair, puffed his pipe, and asked in a tone
of plaintive wonder, "Why is there so much interest in that subject?" I said, maybe it was because the President had said, in a
widely reported chat with White House correspondents that the Attorney General was his "closest adviser," the adviser who was consulted more than any other, "on all legal matters and on many
other matters as well." Mr. Mitchell puffed and ruminated and
murmured, "Did he say that? So *that's* where it started."

A silence ensued. Thinking that a little needling might be useful,
I mentioned a printed account which had him boasting that the
President "hears my views on most important subjects, and I think
he values my judgment." The Attorney General flushed. He
swelled. He rumbled. He said that the account was perfectly ridicu-

"Fits you like a glove!"

A Look at John Mitchell

lous. Nobody in his right mind would believe that he would say such a thing. He would say now what he always said: "In addition to being in the Cabinet, I am on the Urban Affairs Council. The President has asked me to sit with the National Security Council, which I do. I do some work with the national intelligence community." Previous Attorneys General, Secretary of State William P. Rogers and the late Robert Kennedy among them, had sat with the NSC. True enough; but why had the President put him on a special "verification panel" of disarmament and foreign affairs specialists, charged with evaluating the technical factors that may condition American positions to be taken in strategic arms talks with the Soviet Union? "I would presume," Mitchell answered, "that it is because my legal background provides a judgment that isn't provided by the other members. By the nature of that work, you get into a question of proof." Was it true that the President sought his counsel on a comprehensive range of foreign policy questions? "He has asked my opinion on certain matters," Mitchell replied with evident care, adding that "normally, of course, these expressions arise during general discussion with others." Could he, would he cite instances in which it appeared to him that his opinions influenced either foreign or domestic policy decisions? He answered: "I would never know. The President is a man who receives input and advice from many quarters and makes his own determinations. So I wouldn't have the faintest idea of the decisions that I may have influenced."

Change of subject: did he feel that he had been well served, and that he in turn had served the President well, in the background checks that he had been provided and that he in turn had provided the President on Judge Clement Haynsworth, Jr., the South Carolina jurist whose nomination to the Supreme Court had been rejected by the Senate? The opinion that the Attorney General had been badly served by the FBI and by his own staff, and that the President had been badly served by Mitchell, is common in Washington and is shared by some people at the White House. Mitchell said that he disagreed: The President had never expressed dissatisfaction to him; and "I think on balance that the people in this Department and outside provided the background information that was necessary." Labor union pressure and "wild charges," charges that should never have been considered, were "the determining factors."

Now there was another Southern nominee, Harrold Carswell of Georgia and Florida. It had just come out that in a political speech in 1948 he had declared his "firm, vigorous belief in the principles of white supremacy" and had said that "I shall always be so governed." Mitchell said in a formal statement that "a most extensive background investigation" of Judge Carswell "included a complete review of his judicial philosophy and background." He, the Attorney General, remained convinced "that Judge Carswell is firmly committed to the constitutional and moral philosophy of racial equality." I asked Mitchell whether the discovery of the 1948 speech had surprised him. "Yes, it did," he answered. I didn't have to ask him how it was that his investigators had failed to come upon the speech, printed at length at the time in a rural Georgia newspaper edited by Carswell. The oversight was understandable, Mitchell volunteered, "because that newspaper and its records are no longer in existence." The newspaper is defunct, but it was regarded as an official county record and the 1948 files are preserved in the county clerk's office, where a Florida TV reporter found them and the speech. A White House spokesman said that it didn't really matter, anyway: The positions that Judge Carswell took as a young lawyer-editor when he ran for the Georgia legislature in 1948 had been fully covered in the background checks and discounted as the necessary effusions of a deep-South politician at that time. Mitchell put it differently to me: "The information that we had was that he was the most liberal of the three candidates." When he said this, he seemed to be a little shaken, a little uncertain, as if he understood that this latest flaw in his checks upon a Supreme Court nominee was bound to impair his own reputation, whatever effect it might have upon the nominee's chances of confirmation. Evidence that Carswell had been a director, in 1955, of a private club formed in Tallahassee, Florida, in order to take over a city golf course and bar Negroes from it, had not come to light when we had our talk. The Attorney General was preoccupied with happy thoughts of another matter involving Judge Carswell. The judge's critics were going to be confounded, Mitchell said, when they discovered that Carswell had joined in a decision requiring the barbershop where he gets his hair cut to serve Negroes.

Nothing in this encounter shook my previous impressions that Mr. Mitchell wields large influence in both domestic and foreign matters; that the troubles with the Haynsworth and Carswell nomi-

nations are among the many brought upon the Nixon Administration, in part thanks to the Mitchell factor in its affairs, by his and
Mr. Nixon's calculated determination to secure and widen the Administration's hold upon the white Southern vote; and that in numerous respects John Mitchell personifies and encourages some of
the worst tendencies of this Administration.

The Attorney General's conception of himself is fascinating. He
set it forth in a passage that he says he wrote for himself, in a
speech to the American Bar Association in Dallas. His guide as
Attorney General, he said then, "is the ancient common law guide
of the 'reasonable man' whom our forefathers established as the
enlightened compromiser in a pluralistic society. The mark of the
'reasonable man' is to balance the interests; to adhere to a moral
ideal where that adherence is compelling; but, in general, to negotiate a practical middle-of-the-road solution."

How this works out in the Mitchell way was illustrated by his
handling of the electoral reform issue for the President. Nixon said
in one of his first messages to Congress that he favored the direct
election of Presidents but doubted that an amendment providing it
would be ratified by the necessary thirty-eight states. So he, and
Mitchell in his behalf, advocated a proportional method that would
preserve state electors while depriving them of their right to vote
"at whim." Congressman Andrew Jacobs, Jr., of Indiana, asked
Mitchell at a committee hearing why he and Mr. Nixon didn't
"support this principle in which you believe." Mitchell answered,
"It is not a question of the principle we believe in. It is the question
of the proposition that is attainable." The House, contrary to his
and White House calculations, voted for direct election and Nixon
came out for it. Mitchell, who really prefers proportional election,
will be supporting direct election in the Senate this year.

Mitchell denies that he is the principal author of the Administration's substitute for the Voting Rights Act of 1965, though he is.
He also denies that the principal purpose of the substitute is to
please the white South by applying, nationwide, sanctions against
electoral discrimination that now apply only to seven Southern
states. The purpose is all that is seriously wrong with Mitchell's
bill; it preserves the important sanctions, bans literacy tests and
residential requirements (as the US Civil Rights Commission and

the American Civil Liberties Union, among others, have advocated), and probably does not weaken the federal government's
oversight of state and local election laws as gravely as some critics
suspect. Mitchell, tiring of tedious technicalities during the formulation of the bill last year, peremptorily inserted the ban on literacy
tests before he had the facts to support his contention that in many
non-Southern states and cities they discourage minority registration. Now the Civil Rights Commission, not one of his institutional
admirers, has produced some statistics that give his case at least
the color of factual support. But the Southern taint will plague him
in the Senate this year as it did in the House last year. Mr. Nixon's
"reasonable man" will again be reduced to denying the palpable
truth that he and the Administration care less about national electoral fairness than they do about Southern support for Republican
candidates.

An organization that made this point with telling force is the
Ripon Society, an aggregation of relatively progressive and mostly
young Republicans. Three of its former officers are on Nixon's
White House staff. Mitchell, stung by Ripon's criticism, blurted
into a TV microphone that its members are so many "little juvenile
delinquents." It was hardly the remark of a truly "reasonable
man," but it has been noted to his credit at the White House that he
has not had the delinquents fired, as he probably could do if he put
his mind and his influence with Mr. Nixon to it.

Two similar variations from what is widely thought to be the
Mitchell norm are noteworthy. His assent was decisive in the Administration's successful effort to eliminate from a new tax act a
provision that would have deprived the Southern Regional Council
of the foundation money it uses to further Negro voter registration.
The other variation had to do with the November, 1969, Mobiliza-
tion against the Vietnam war, which drove Mitchell to excesses of
misrepresentation and indirect repression. He got a notion that
Richard Blumenthal, a bright Democrat on the Nixon staff, was a
Mobe spy within the Nixon house and marked him for imminent
dismissal. Then along came Donald Rumsfeld, the poverty director, with a recommendation that Blumenthal be appointed, at age
23, the head of VISTA, the poverty program's domestic Peace
Corps. Mitchell calmed down, heard out Blumenthal's explanation
that he was only communicating with the Mobe leadership for the
White House, and said he wouldn't oppose the appointment. It's

the sort of thing that causes the minority of moderate men around Mr. Nixon to believe that there's good in and hope for John Mitchell, after all.

February 7, 1970

III

Birth
of a Budget

Around noon of January 3, 1970, a reporter and Henry A. Kissinger, the President's foreign policy man, were chatting on the sunny patio outside Kissinger's office at the California White House when Press Secretary Ronald Ziegler emerged from an adjoining office. Ziegler stared for a moment at the visitor and then, with a look of consternation so extreme that the reporter thought he must be kidding, whirled and dashed back into the office from which he had come, slamming the door behind him as he vanished. There, it developed later, he told H. R. (Bob) Haldeman and John Ehrlichman, the President's chief domestic assistants, that disaster was upon them. They had been talking over the final, secret figures of the Nixon budget for fiscal 1971 and, through the open door of the office, the reporter must have heard it all. Mr. Nixon is no man to tolerate leaks of that magnitude, accidental or not, and his prospective wrath was too awful for contemplation.

It was well for the reporter that he had heard none of the budget

talk, for he would have looked the fool afterward if he had taken
the figures of early January as seriously as the President and the
few officials who were privy to them did. After months of arduous
study and review, and a last round of conferences with Budget Director Robert P. Mayo in California, the President had approved
on that morning a 1971 budget—firm, sound, solid, and balanced
were the descriptives favored by his staff—that called for spending
some $205 billion in the next fiscal year. Increased excise taxes
and accelerated collection of estate taxes would, if voted by Congress, provide $3.2 billion of new revenue and a surplus of better
than $2 billion. Mr. Nixon was said to be immensely pleased with
his work. Projected defense spending was down, social spending
was up, and the intended surplus, while smaller than he would have
liked, stamped it as a mildly anti-inflationary budget. Expecting
approval and applause from a valued quarter, he placed a telephone call from California to Arthur F. Burns in Washington. The
results of the call, soon to be apparent, are recited with pride at the
White House now, but they seem to me to bring the boasted sure-
ness and efficiency of the Nixon decision process into question.

The budgetary views of Arthur Burns, a conservative economist
and White House Counselor who was about to become chairman
of the Federal Reserve Board, were already known to the President. Throughout the previous months of preparation, Burns had
urged upon Nixon the absolute necessity of a 1971 budget that
promised a believable surplus of revenue over expenditure and did
not depend for that result upon fiscal tricks, congressional vagary,
and the imponderables that tend to make every Presidential budget
a chancy exercise. Only a genuine surplus and stringently restrained expenditure, Burns had argued, would convince the public,
the business community, Congress, and his prospective colleagues
on the Federal Reserve Board that the Administration was as determined as it said it was to check inflation. The FRB was especially important because the President counted on it, under Burns'
chairmanship, for the gradual relaxation of recent credit and monetary restrictions that was thought necessary if the rate of inflation
was to be diminished without a severe recession. How, given all
this, Mr. Nixon could have been surprised and set a-back by Burns'
response when he heard about the "final" budget decisions is puzzling, but he was. Burns said in his growly way, by telephone and
after the President returned to Washington, that the adopted

budget would not do. It turned upon the doubtful willingness of Congress to enact new taxes in an election year, just after it had voted income-tax cuts that far exceeded Nixon's wishes. The whole thing was slippery, tricky, too uncertain, smacking of a scheme to put congressional Democrats on the hook and relieve the Administration of responsibility for an inflationary rather than a counter-inflationary budget.

Enter George Romney, the Secretary of Housing and Urban Development. He was worried about the shrinkage of credit for housing, the inflated interest rates that added to costs, and the generally dimming prospects that the ambitious targets he had set for new housing could be met. Also, for a man who had been the Governor of Michigan and had hoped to be President, the first Nixon year had not been a happy one. Some of his proposed programs had been questioned and cut up by more favored Presidential advisers. He was counted, perhaps unfairly, among the least effective Cabinet members. It happened that he had an appointment with Burns on the Sunday after Nixon called Burns from California. Romney and Burns found themselves in perfect agreement about the Nixon budget and about its predictable effect upon housing, among other things, if it was not so reconstructed that credit sources could be expanded and interest rates could be lowered. That could be accomplished only if federal expenditures were brought within the limits of foreseeable revenue, minus the problematical tax increases recommended in the Nixon version. Romney alone could hardly have persuaded the President to alter a course that seemed to be firmly set. Even Burns, with his greater standing and influence, probably could not have. Together they prevailed and, incidentally, provided George Romney with his finest hour in Washington.

It occurred at an extraordinary Cabinet session convened by Nixon after he returned from California and had been exposed in private to the Burns and Romney arguments. Only Cabinet members were present, without the usual array of assistants. Nixon opened it by introducing Romney, with the announcement that he had something important to say. Romney said it, concluding with an offer to cut the HUD budget of about $3.5 billion, as it then stood, by five percent or $170 million. Nixon, in the manner of a pastor calling upon the faithful for contributions, challenged the other Cabinet heads to do likewise. They did and the consequence, after a fortnight of frantic review by agency staffs and the Budget Bureau, was the $202 billion budget with a precarious $1.3 billion surplus that the President submitted to Congress on February 2.

Naturally enough, stories told of Nixon's own performance before and during the final stage—or "ratchet," as people in the Budget Bureau call each successive phase of fiscal evolution—do him maximum credit. But they are interesting, if for nothing more than their indication of the way he is viewed by his assistants. They say, for instance, that he insisted upon retaining through the final round some previously accepted increases in funds for heart, cancer, and dental research. One of the more surprising items in a Nixon budget, a $17 million increase (to $40 million) in funds for the National Foundation on the Arts and Humanities, is attributed to the intervention of Leonard Garment, a former Nixon law partner who joined the White House staff in mid-1969 and endeavors in every way he can to improve the Presidential image among people who value the arts. It also is said that the President worked terribly hard on the budget and enjoyed every minute of it. A story told in support of this point has him laboring at 11:30 on a recent night with William Safire, one of his speech and message writers, when Robert Mayo appeared, announcing happily that he had found another soft spot in the space agency's budget. The President shooed Safire from the office and an hour later, well past midnight, was still grinding away at the soft spot with Mayo. The submitted space budget for 1971 turned out to be $486 million lower than the one for fiscal 1970.

The President is said to attach maximum importance to a budget corollary that received very little notice. This was his undertaking, in the annual economic message that accompanied his budget message, to "appoint a commission to study our financial structure and make recommendations to me for needed changes." Congressman Wright Patman of Texas, a dedicated critic of the Federal Reserve System, and of banking practices, suspected that this was just a device to postpone action on a pending proposal to ban one-bank holding companies. Not so, say Nixon associates who have discussed the need for such a study with the President. According to them, it is intended to be a serious though unobtrusive review of financial premises that have prevailed since the Federal Reserve System was established in 1914. It is said to reflect Mr. Nixon's conviction that the country's monetary and credit system simply is not working as it should and that it requires major changes. His commission study could be, in the long run, more important than the budget that he approved in January and the quite different one that he sent to Congress.

February 14, 1970

———

A deficit many times bigger than the one foreseen in early 1970 was in prospect in early 1971. A year after the President ordered it, nothing more had been heard of the financial study.

"'FIX' DOESN'T NECESSARILY MEAN 'REPAIR.'"

I V

Chicken, Southern Fried

"Okay," said the Nixon man, "so we laid the egg and then we had to build the chicken."

The egg was Vice President Spiro T. Agnew's disclosure February 1, on CBS's *Face the Nation,* that the President had decided to appoint "a Cabinet-level group" to guide and comfort the South through the agonies of integrating its segregated public schools without any more of the delay that parts of it have been getting away with since 1954. The chicken that had to be "built" was not so much the group itself as a decent and believable definition of what it is supposed to accomplish and of how that is to be done. This turned out to be oddly difficult, considering the fact that the President himself intended to announce his decision to establish the Cabinet group at his press conference on the preceding Friday. He left the honor to Agnew because nobody asked Nixon for his reaction to the Supreme Court's series of rulings in late 1969 to the effect that after February 1 only completely integrated and "unitary" school systems would be acceptable. "This is something," Press Secretary Ronald Ziegler said the day after Agnew said the President would "shortly announce" his decision, "that the President has had in mind ever since the Supreme Court established the law." He meant, since October 29, when the Supreme Court astounded the Administration and Attorney General John N. Mitchell by holding that the time for "all deliberate speed" in school integration had ended and that "the obligation of every school district is to terminate dual school systems at once."

The Attorney General had assumed and had led the President to assume, as Mitchell said later in an interview, that "the Court would respect the Administration's wishes" for some further delay in the 40 Mississippi, Louisiana, and South Carolina cases before it, and then for continuing judicial recognition that true integration of historically segregated school systems is a hard and complicated task. This assumption underlay Mitchell's basic doctrine, which he formulated and expressed (to me, among others) before Nixon was elected, that as a matter both of political wisdom and of constitutional propriety, the courts rather than the Executive branch of the federal government should bear the burden and onus of enforcing racial integration of public schools in the South and—if it came to that—elsewhere. In accordance with his view, the Attorney General brought about a rapid and major shift of enforcement responsibility from the Department of Health, Education, and Welfare to the Justice Department and, through Justice, to the federal courts. It was in the knowledge that this would happen if he were elected that Nixon encouraged Southern segregationists to believe in 1968 that they could expect at least as much sympathy and protection from him in the White House as they were promised by his third-party rival, George C. Wallace. As Wallace is saying now, the Southerners who fell for this aspect of Nixon's "Southern strategy" were thoroughly deceived. Attorney General Mitchell has run up a good record of enforcement, better than he is generally given credit for and better in some respects than that of his Democratic predecessors. But his actions have been rooted in the assumption described—that the federal courts and especially the Supreme Court, with a Nixon Chief Justice at its head, would hold short of the demand for integration "at once" that the Court proclaimed in October and sustained in several subsequent decisions.

It follows that the White House was no better prepared than the

recalcitrant South was for the situation in which Mr. Nixon and his
Southern friends find themselves. Given the record of equivocation
that he had behind him when he took office, and the disgraceful
continuance of it through much of 1969 by HEW Secretary Robert
Finch and the Attorney General (in their spoken pronouncements
as distinct from their official actions), the President is in a poor
position to ask for the belief in his good faith in setting up his
Cabinet group that the subordinates working on it for him do ask.

Certain accompanying circumstances do not improve Mr.
Nixon's position. Agnew, who is to be the group's chairman, said
that it was being established "for the purpose of implementing the
decisions of the Court in the least disruptive way to quality education in the South." How is this to be done if Presidential mediators
are not to take a hand in HEW and Justice enforcement and compliance procedures, if the Cabinet group is not to become in effect
"a point of appeal" for aggrieved segregators? One is asked to
believe that the Cabinet group will not do that and won't be that.
Senator Strom Thurmond, the South Carolina Republican who
did much in 1968 to persuade the lower South, on Nixon's behalf, that its white segregationists could expect sympathy and
help from President Nixon, recommended to the White House
"the creation of a Presidential commission to study the effects
of court-ordered integration" well before Agnew announced the
intention. One is asked to believe that the White House assistants
who developed the idea with Mr. Nixon and are implementing
it for him—among them being Special Counsel Harry Dent, Thurmond's former assistant—didn't know that Thurmond had said
a word to anybody at the White House about it. Senator John
Stennis of Mississippi, leading an effort to frighten non-Southern
Senators into lightening integrationist pressure upon the South by
demanding that the same pressure be applied everywhere, found
the President's move "a very significant thing" and said "It is none
too soon." Senator John McClellan of Arkansas wanted to know,
"What power does the panel have to modify the impact of recent
Supreme Court decisions?" and suggested that if it is to have no
such power "this is just another gesture." Senator Fritz Hollings,
Thurmond's moderate Democratic colleague, skeptically recommended that Agnew and his group favor segregated Northern
rather than Southern schools with their attention, and Congressman
John R. Rarick of Louisiana saw in the whole thing a "new rape

of the South." But Southern Congressmen mostly welcomed it with an enthusiasm that Mr. Nixon, longing to be thought only in pursuit of ways to maintain "quality education" in integrated schools, could not have relished.

The fact is, given the Supreme Court's current stand, no Presidential group, commission, or committee—the style of it was yet to be determined on February 11—can be an effective "point of appeal" or do much more than rally whatever enlightened community support there may be in the beleaguered school districts for compliance with declared law. The identities of the two men upon whom the President principally relied to build his chicken for him are also reassuring. One of them is Mr. Nixon's (and Mr. Mitchell's) former law partner, Leonard Garment, a White House assistant charged with staff oversight of racial and integregationist matters. If Len Garment cannot be trusted to act in good faith in such an endeavor, nobody at the Nixon White House can be. The other man in the hatchery is Secretary of Labor George Shultz, who is to be the Cabinet group's vice chairman.

The day after Agnew disclosed the plan, in terms said to be substantially inaccurate, the President assigned Shultz to do for this project essentially what he did the preceding summer for the Administration's welfare reforms. That was to closet himself with a mass of documented alternative approaches and come up with a workable synthesis of what was wanted and what was practicable. He reported his findings on the following Saturday, at a meeting of designated Cabinet members and staff assistants (while Agnew, the front-man chairman, was in California, playing golf with Bob Hope and beaning a touring professional). The thrust of Shultz's synthesis was that the Cabinet group should stay clear of enforcement and complaints about it; capitalize to the limit upon Attorney General Mitchell's and Vice President Agnew's ill-won but useful standing with white Southerners; and—as Garment also recommended—put big money and real effort into generating support for and compliance with the law and court requirements in the afflicted states. It was recognized, with something less than total happiness, that the Administration was abandoning the Mitchell strategy of leaving the political onus with the courts. In effect, Mr. Nixon was asked to take a chance that compliance with the law and elemental decency may be the best politics open to him now.

February 21, 1970

V

Agnew's Effect

They no longer pretend at the White House that Vice President Spiro T. Agnew speaks only for himself and not for Mr. Nixon. Reporters who are foolish enough to ask for it are told the old lie, in a half-hearted way, but they are not expected to believe it. Agnew himself says that "the President and I talk—not what you would call frequently, not on a daily basis, but frequently enough that I am aware of any departures in his thinking that might affect what I say." Nixon's speech writers prize and acknowledge their assignments to draft Agnew speeches. Patrick Buchanan deplores reports that he has written some of the more abrasive ones, not because the reports are false, but because Agnew resents any indication that he is a mouthpiece for others and the stories might impair a working relationship that Buchanan and his colleagues have come to value. Another Nixon writer, William Safire, suffered the pains of a neglected author when the national press ignored one of Agnew's accounts, delivered in California, of his recent tour through Asia. The President sent him on that trip with a warm expression of confidence, welcomed him home with pride, and then dispatched him around the country to explain his explanation to Asians of "the Nixon doctrine." This simple task requires the Vice

FLIGHT OF THE BUMBLEBEE

President to say, with homey embellishments, that the United States intends to involve itself less in the world at less cost to itself while maintaining the involvements. Agnew's way of saying this goes over well and he is thought at the White House to have conducted both the trip and his subsequent promotion of it as a major contribution to US foreign policy with laudable aplomb.

Agnew evidently agrees. Since his return, his show of confidence in himself and in his standing with the President is formidable. He fielded with total composure the suggestion on a recent television program that he just might displace Nixon as the Republican candidate for President in 1972 ("it would be ridiculous") and said with equal calm that he wouldn't rule out running for the Presidency in 1976. The fact that he has risen since October from national ridicule to national acclaim upon the backs of sundry effete snobs, self-styled intellectuals, New Leftists, and dissident riffraff does not disturb him any more than it appears to disturb Mr. Nixon —which is to say, not at all. As they say at the White House, why should it? At the last over-all count, through January, Agnew had received 149,000 letters and telegrams in less than four months and all but 10,000 of them approved of him and of what he had been saying. Now, after his detour into foreign statesmanship, he is back to saying the same things with modifications that are not really modifications but subtle reiterations of the themes that have aroused precisely the responses that he and the President intended to arouse. They count upon the responses from "the great silent majority" and from their "Middle America" of frustrated and embittered citizens to win congressional seats and governorships for the Republicans in 1970 and to win the Presidency again in 1972, by a solid majority vote rather than by the minority that elected Nixon and Agnew in 1968.

One of the themes was and still is the attack upon all news media and the threat to the federally licensed media of radio and television that Agnew began late in 1969 with his speeches at Des Moines and Montgomery. In this he has been and still is greatly assisted by the attacked media, their masochistic drivel to the effect that he merely raised legitimate questions about news coverage and commentary, and the fatuous acceptance of his recent assertion in Baltimore that he was "calling off the war." That was the concluding

line of a speech in which he said that he was happy to be back home
at "my favorite time of the year in Maryland, that wonderful time
when the Sunpapers are on strike" (the *Baltimore Sun,* morning
and evening, had been shut by a pressmen's strike since January 2).
He said in a spitting shout that the same papers disposed of their
garbage by printing it, salted in a crack at the "guerrilla theater" of
blacks and antiwar people who were demonstrating outside the
hall, and preceded his closing line about calling off the war with the
remark that "I have a great respect for the free media." The free
media reported with supine absence of comment his boast—a boast
that comes over to me from my tape recorder in a tone of gloating
malice—that "somehow when I look around the tube from time to
time, I feel that I've had a modicum of success here and there."

Agnew meant that he feels, as do many others at the White
House, that television in particular treats him and the Administration generally with more care, that it carries more conservative and
therefore friendly comment or non-comment on Administration
pronouncements, than it did before he opened up on it with his
brutal reminders that it is a licensed business. On *Face the Nation*
the following Sunday, he was handled with great gentility by two
CBS men and a magazine reporter. "I'm sorry, I didn't mean to put
you on the spot," George Herman of CBS said in apology for one
of the tougher questions, none of which was very tough. The panel-
ists let him get by, as reporters generally have done, with his irrelevant claim that he has not been "advocating censorship," which he
and the federal government have no power to impose. They didn't
ask him whether he has been practicing intimidation, which he as
Vice President does have the power to do and has been doing and
is still doing. They didn't ask him, either, whether he intends to
resume "the war" when and if he chooses. I asked that question at
the White House and was told by Agnew's press spokesman, Herbert Thompson, that the Vice President is prepared to resume it
and will resume it whenever and if he considers that "the situation
requires it."

A fallout response to his attacks upon the news media and upon
the "whole zoo" of American dissent is perfectly apparent to
Agnew, to others at the White House, and to the President. This is
the extraordinary volume and virulence of the expressions of hates
and antipathies that his performance has evoked. Much of it—
some of it directly to Agnew, more of it to broadcasters, commen-

tators, publishers, public speakers who differ in the slightest with
him and with what he is understood to be saying—takes the form
of the most atrocious racism, including anti-Semitism. The day before this was written, a Washington station that had dared to interview a militant black professor in California was denounced for
"throwing shit in the face of us Caucasians" by a letter writer who
cited Agnew in support of his view. Norman Isaacs of Louisville,
the President of the American Society of Newspaper Editors, has
reported to Herbert Klein, the President's director of communications, the anti-Semitic filth that he draws with his speeches de-
nouncing what he considers to be the Vice President's blatant
threats against the licensed news media. "My God," Isaacs recalls
Klein saying in reply, "those people are kooks. They don't represent America." Granted. But they consider that Agnew represents
them and speaks for them, and they tell Agnew so. His staff
spokesmen say that he has been surprised and deeply distressed by
this part of the response he elicits. He is also said to reply only in
the most formal terms to the many complaints he receives against
news media and commentators, some addressed directly to him and
some marked "Copy to the Vice President." But, his meaningless
suspension of "the war" aside, he has done nothing whatever to
moderate or alter the line of talk that draws the response and in
fact has stepped up its intensity and frequency.

   Eric Sevareid of CBS is one of the many commentators who do
not agree that they have consciously moderated their handling of
Administration and other news, including the news that Agnew
makes, but do feel that they are forced to function in an atmosphere of public and official surveillance. The atmosphere is attended by such events as a Washington, D.C., educational station's
cancellation of a critical teleview of the Vietnam war, and by the
sudden effort of a group including several Nixon friends and former
business associates to snatch a Miami television station away from
the *Washington Post-Newsweek* organization, one of Agnew's particular targets and one at which he is still taking pot-shots. In an
interview Sevareid said that he felt as if Agnew had thrown "a pail
of garbage" at him, and he set forth a theory that may explain the
Agnew performance in part. Discrediting the media, he said, could
be "one way for a government to protect itself from having its own
credibility gap." It also could be, though I have little hope that it
will be, one way for this Administration to create its own credibil-

ity gap. Agnew raised that hope when he said, in one of his characteristic assays at sweet reason: "You cannot build an enduring
majority in this country by appealing to passions and prejudices
that contradict the best and most basic ideals of its people. And the
Republican Party of Richard Nixon does not intend to try."

February 28, 1970

———

George Herman of CBS pointed out to me later that he did not
apologize to Agnew for the substance of a question, but for putting
a difficult question in the closing seconds of the program.

V I

Sham
or Surrender

It was 7 P.M. on February 23 and time for Harry Dent to get back
to his work at the White House, after 90 minutes of the kind of
easy talk he loves, when I said to him in parting: "If what you have
been telling me is correct, a lot of people in the South are going to
wake up one day soon and realize that this Administration has
double-crossed them." Harry laughed and said that he didn't think
so. What he had been telling me was correct, nobody was being
double-crossed, and—with soft and friendly emphasis: "You tell
your Atlanta friend that I think he's wrong."

The Atlanta friend is Paul Anthony, executive director of the
Southern Regional Council. He and Harry Dent are very different
white men: Anthony working with the Council for racial integration in every phase of the region's life because he thinks it is right;
and Dent, sometime assistant to Senator Strom Thurmond of South
Carolina and now the President's Special Counsel and political coordinator, working (he really does) to reconcile the South to a
necessary minimum of integration because he thinks it is inevitable
and in the Republican interest. I had talked to Anthony by telephone from Washington that afternoon and (without naming him)
had quoted the gist of what he said to Dent. "There is just the most

"HE LIKES MY GRITS."

widespread feeling down here," Paul Anthony said, "from black militants right across the board to segregationist whites, that the white South is winning this thing and that the Nixon Administration has turned its back on desegregation." White "liberals"— politicians, businessmen, editors, community leaders of every sort —were running for cover. "Nigra" and "nigger" were suddenly back in style among upper-class whites who had been training themselves for years to say "Neegro" and "black" (bless that word, so easy to pronounce). There was outspoken satisfaction, among segregationists and professed integrationists alike, that so many blacks were coming to their senses and seeing that integration, especially in the public schools, wasn't all that it had been cracked up to be and beginning to fight to keep their black schools black. "And they're saying these things to me," Paul Anthony said, speaking of some of his white acquaintances, and "assuming that of course I agree with them." This, to him, was conclusive evidence that the positions taken by the Nixon Administration and in Congress in the past few weeks had profoundly changed the Southern scene.

Not so, said Harry Dent. If all that was happening, if that feeling about the Nixon Administration existed in the South, it was based on a big misunderstanding. The President's policy on the racial integration of public schools had not changed at all, and there were not going to be "any big changes" in that regard in the South or anywhere else. Everybody down there, in his own South Carolina and the rest of the South, understood by now that the law and the court orders had to be enforced and were going to be enforced. Maybe with "a little more understanding" of the difficulties, more sympathy, "better communication"—but enforced all the same. That was what Vice President Agnew's Cabinet committee on integration was all about. It was true that he, Harry Dent, had suggested that the President create some kind of committee or commission to study the effects of required integration as it had been applied up to that time in the South, and recommend ways to make the process easier for all concerned. But it was news to him that his old patron, Senator Thurmond, had suggested the same thing to the White House at about the same time; the Senator must have done it through Bryce Harlow, the President's chief communicator with Congress. The only man he knew of around the White House who had made a similar suggestion was Leonard Garment (this with a kindly smile, saying without saying that I knew as well as he did that Len Garment is regarded by people like me as one of the few approximately kindred souls on the White House staff). The idea for the Cabinet committee—the President officially dubbed it "an informal Cabinet-level working group"—had emerged, so far as Harry knew, from the office of John Ehrlichman, the Assistant for Domestic Affairs.

How was the Agnew group going "to review in detail," as the President had put it, "the efforts of the Executive Branch" to further compliance with integration laws and court orders without getting into the hair of the people who were supposed to be enforcing them at the Departments of Justice and Health, Education, and Welfare? And what could the Cabinet group really do in and for a county like Darlington, in Harry's South Carolina—where the school authorities had been ordered by the courts to integrate now and where the whites had boycotted the schools—except try somehow to take the heat off? Well now, said Harry, those were good questions and he didn't know the answers and he doubted that anybody else at the White House did—yet. But there would be answers, and they wouldn't be the kind of answers that my Atlanta friend and, according to him, a lot of other people in the South were expecting.

I asked Harry, in his capacity as one of Mr. Nixon's certified political experts, whether I was right or wrong in my impression that the establishment of the Agnew group and everything else that had happened in this area recently, including the President's qualified but at the same time "full support" of the Stennis amendment calling for uniform application of integration laws in the South and everywhere else, was in fact a political response to a political problem. Dent knew what I had in mind: the Supreme Court's recent demand that school segregation by law and deliberate official action be ended now, once and for all, and the outraged Southern reaction that in turn had revived George C. Wallace's hottest issue and lent fearsome force to his threat that Nixon would not carry a single Southern state in 1972 unless he began to "do right" by the South. Why, yes—Harry answered—of course there was a political problem and of course it had to be dealt with and was being dealt with. But that didn't mean that the law and the court orders were not going to be enforced. What it really meant was that this Administration was determined to enforce them in such a way as to get the problem over with, get it solved and out of the way, not only before 1972 but by the fall of 1970, before the congressional and state elections. If I didn't believe it, ask John Mitchell. That was what the Attorney General had been saying at the White House, in the discussions preceding the formation of the Agnew group and the various statements on the Stennis and other integration amendments: get that problem solved, get it out of our way, and the only way to do that was to enforce the law in a way that the South would understand and accept. It could be done and it was going to be done. "You'll see," Harry said.

What I and everybody else actually saw, among other things not quite according to Harry's script, was the summary firing of Leon Panetta, HEW's chief integration enforcer, and the selection of one of his determined foes in that department, General Counsel Robert C. Mardian, to be the staff director of the Agnew Cabinet group. In obedience to the President's directive, he is the man who is to "review in detail" the enforcement practices and policies of Justice and HEW. In doing so Mardian is bound to oversee Panetta's successor in a fashion and to an extent that HEW Secretary Finch never allowed him to do. Mardian makes splendid speeches, all about the duty of school authorities to enforce integration and break up deliberate segregation. He told Louisiana school board members in January that integrated education is "as American as apple pie." Panetta, Commissioner of Education James E. Allen, and some others who had to work with him at HEW didn't care for Mardian's pie. Mardian recommended in March of 1969, in a secret memorandum that ceased to be secret, that the department relax its strict school guidelines without announcing it and so avoid a fuss. He has been heard to say in department meetings, too often for the comfort of officials dedicated to real enforcement, "Now don't get me wrong, I'm not for segregation" and, "Now don't get me wrong, I'm for Negroes and equal rights." His HEW associates, those who agreed with him and those who disagreed, didn't get him wrong and one may doubt that the White House people who chose him for the Agnew staff job got him wrong, either. He is there to do the job that Paul Anthony in Atlanta and Southerners everywhere now know is going to be done.

March 7, 1970

VII

A Faithful Servant

The measure of Daniel P. Moynihan's value to the President that other White House assistants favor when they discuss him nowadays is no longer, as it was for a time, that he is the senior Democrat and liberal in Mr. Nixon's service. Moynihan remains a Democrat by affiliation, but his associates have every reason to gather that he sets no great store by the "liberal" tag. His strictures upon what he calls "the liberal establishment," recognized members of it, and the "myths" to which he thinks they adhere with blind persistence, are so stringent and so frequent as to set him apart from the establishment and to identify him, in the minds and talk of his White House fellows, with those among them whose great virtue and value is that they know how to serve Richard Nixon and how, in serving him, to be effective with him. It is said of Pat Moynihan now that he is a superb bureaucrat, the perfect assistant and Counselor (his current title), who in his first 13 months at the White

House has proven himself a master of the difficult art of serving a President without reducing the servant to utter servility.

It is in this light that the inquirer at the White House is encouraged to read an example of Moynihan's counsel to the President that the *New York Times* published on March 1. In a 1600-word memorandum that Moynihan typed for himself and dated January 16, he offered the President "a general assessment of the position of Negroes at the end of the first year of your Administration, and of the decade in which their position has been the central domestic political issue." On February 10 the President's staff manager, H. R. Haldeman, had copies of the hitherto private memorandum distributed to Vice President Agnew, four Cabinet members, and three White House assistants. This normally happens only when the President orders it done, and Moynihan agreed the other day that it is "a fair assumption" that the President ordered the distribution in this case. Moynihan also said that he had been expecting the memorandum to be leaked to the press ever since he learned of the distribution. He said that he thought to himself, "Oh God, this is it," when Peter Kihss of the *Times* caught him by telephone on Saturday, February 28, just as he was about to leave for a flight to Antigua (where he persuaded ex-Defense Secretary Neil McElroy, the Procter and Gamble soap chairman, to head up a new commission that will study the problems of educational finance). Kihss told Moynihan that the *Times* had the full text, and Moynihan urged him to print the whole if he printed anything.

Moynihan and others at the White House prefer to believe that the document was leaked from one of the departments whose Secretaries received it. The suspected department is Health, Education, and Welfare, where Secretary Robert H. Finch permitted wide distribution to his subordinates. One of the several who received copies was Leon Panetta, director of the Office for Civil Rights, who was fired shortly afterward at Nixon's personal order. "That is completely false," Panetta says of the supposition at the White House that he did the foul deed. Photocopies were all over the place within a matter of days, and the sufficient certainty is that somebody who saw a chance to discredit Moynihan and/or the Administration's racial and civil rights policies passed the memo to the *Times*.

The publication served that purpose, but the point of lasting in-

terest in the episode is the light the affair throws upon Nixon and
the Nixon White House. Here Pat Moynihan was addressing a
man, the President, with whom he had been in continuous dialogue
for more than a year. One of the two central points of the memorandum—that "the American Negro is making extraordinary progress"—could not in itself have been news to Mr. Nixon, who often
said as much during his 1968 campaign and has relied upon the
belief that it is so during his Presidency. The statistics used to document the point were derived, accurately so far as they went, from
an interim Census Bureau study that Moynihan had largely in-
spired. Census and Labor Department statisticians who prepared
the source report quarreled seriously with only one assertion in the
Moynihan document—that "outside the South, young husband-
wife Negro families have 99 percent of the income of whites."
Moynihan should have noted, the statisticians thought, that this
was true of only 135,000 out of 1.5 million non-Southern Negro
families. The professionals added with less emphasis that Moynihan might also have noted such other qualifying facts as that in a
typical mid-income category (around $7000) it took three earners
in a Negro family to equal the income of one earner in a compara-
ble white family. But balance of that kind was not what Moynihan
was after. Why bore and burden his President with qualifying negatives in presenting what he considered to be a useful and effective
positive point, one that was bound to reassure Mr. Nixon that he
was right in his present assumptions and in the course of action and
non-action that the assumptions indicate?

The dynamite passage in the memo, the one that caused Moynihan to say "Oh, God" to himself when it got out, was that "The
time may have come when the issue of race could benefit from a
period of 'benign neglect.' " My reading of it and of the section it
introduced is exactly what Moynihan since has insisted that he intended to imply: nothing more or less than that such Administration figures as Attorney General Mitchell and Vice President
Agnew should be made to stop providing "opportunities for mar-
tyrdom, heroics, histrionics or whatever" to Black Panthers, people
like the defendants in the Chicago conspiracy trial, and kindred
"hysterics, paranoiacs, and boodlers" on both sides of the explo-
sive racial and social issues of the day. But his way of putting it in
the memorandum and of justifying it later invited the distortion it
received, to the effect that he was recommending "benign neglect"

of the entire racial problem. On the day before the document was published, Moynihan had brought the President together in privacy, for several hours of intimate discussion of that problem among others, with a group that included Professor Charles V. Hamilton of Columbia University, a renowned black advocate of reasoned militance, David Riesman and James Wilson of Harvard, and others to whom the thought of "benign neglect" would be anathema. Moynihan at that meeting was serving his purpose, and a useful one it is, of the Presidential educator, exposing Mr. Nixon to talk and views of a kind that are new to him and could be as valuable to the country as the President is said to think they are to him.

There is no reason to doubt that Counselor Moynihan is riding high. He is occupied with projects ranging from the reduction of illegal heroin imports to a depth study of national economic growth and the directions it ought to take. It is accepted at the White House that Moynihan will be leaving the Nixon service at the end of 1970, returning to his professorship at Harvard. But not, it is quite clear, because of any unhappiness with the uglier aspects of the Nixon course, including the ones that he touched obliquely upon in the published memo. A necessity of the assistant's art is that nothing be allowed to distract the assistant from his particular concerns and service. Pat Moynihan is as good at that part of it as he is still thought to be at the whole art of serving a President.

March 14, 1970

"PERSONALLY, I'D JUST AS SOON GIVE UP DOMINOES AND GO BACK TO CRAPS."

VIII

Lousing Up Laos

Enormous care and effort went into the preparation of the "precise description of our current activities in Laos" that Mr. Nixon submitted to the American public on March 6. He got the assent of the National Security Council to a degree of disclosure that he and two of his predecessors, Presidents Kennedy and Johnson, had not previously considered to be in the national interest. Nixon then assigned to his assistant for national security affairs, Henry A. Kissinger, the task of making certain that the disclosure was in fact precise if not complete, wholly credible, beyond any possible criticism on the grounds of inaccuracy or deceit. Kissinger undertook the task with characteristic and ferocious zeal. He warned the Departments of State and Defense, the military services, the CIA, the aid agency, the several subagencies that participate in clandestine operations in Vietnam and Laos, that the officials who provided him with requested data would be fired if any of the information turned out to be incomplete, inaccurate, or misleading in any way. Every American who could be fairly said to be "stationed in Laos" was to be identified, his or her activities were to be precisely defined, and military operations, air and ground, conducted in and over Laos were to be reported to him in equally meticulous detail.

Kissinger and his staff had access to the secret testimony recently taken by Senator Stuart Symington's subcommittee on the Laos involvement, and took special care that the figures and assertions of fact incorporated in the Nixon statement should conform with the Symington record, when and if a sanitized version of it is published.

Equal care attended certain corollaries. The one new and positive action that the President and his advisers could think of, apart from the factual disclosure, was an appeal to Soviet Premier Kosygin to join British Prime Minister Wilson in working with other signatories of the 1962 Geneva Accords for restoration of the terms that then, in theory, guaranteed the peace and neutrality of Laos. Wilson and Prime Minister Souvanna Phouma of Laos had already made the same request, without effect. The United States had previously refused to formally join or support such requests to the Soviet Government, in connection with the Laos and Vietnam conflicts, in the belief that the Soviets would refuse and that it was idle to waste what goodwill there was between Washington and Moscow on a predictably vain gesture. Given the present decision to make the gesture, the normal course would have been to forewarn the Soviet Government of the public announcement. This was not done before the morning of March 6 because, if the request had been privately rejected before it was announced, the President could not have opened his Laos statement, as he did, with his one and only show of positive action for peace in Laos.

Much thought also went into the form of the announcement and the extent to which Nixon would personally identify himself with it. He could have delivered the whole on national television, as he did his November 3 speech on Vietnam. He could have recorded and filmed parts of it for radio and television, as he sometimes does with quite minor statements. He did neither. He postponed the statement until he had arrived and was settled at his Florida retreat on Key Biscayne for a long (Friday-Sunday) weekend. He remained in seclusion when his staff issued a written statement in his name and followed it with the kind of special, though by now hardly unusual, background briefing at which reporters are exposed to the guidance and wisdom of the highest available "White House officials." The reporters present are not supposed to translate this into "White House official," but some do.

The central purpose of the statement and of the supplementary briefing was to put to rest "grossly inaccurate" reports and "intense public speculation" to the effect that "the United States involvement in Laos has substantially increased in violation of the Geneva Accords, that American ground forces are engaged in combat in Laos and that our air activity has had the effect of escalating the conflict." Mr. Nixon acknowledged that "our air activity" has increased, both to inhibit North Vietnam's reinforcement of its units in South Vietnam over the Ho Chi Minh trails through northern Laos, and in direct support of Laotian government forces fighting North Vietnamese and Laotian Communist forces in Laos. This the United States would continue to do, along with the supply, training, and field support of "regular and irregular Laotian forces" so long as this was "necessary to protect American lives in Vietnam and to preserve a precarious but important balance in Laos" —and also necessary, the President said, "to prevent the recognized Laotian government from being overwhelmed by larger Communist forces dominated by the North Vietnamese." But the major intent of his statement and of the briefer's amplication was to minimize the American involvement in ground combat in Laos. Of a total of 1040 Americans stationed in Laos, in direct government employ or on contract, 320 were military advisers and trainers, 323 were suppliers, and (the briefer said) a little over 200 of these were military personnel. Three sentences in the Nixon statement drove home the point: "There are no American ground combat troops in Laos. We have no plans for introducing ground combat forces into Laos," and—in an assertion that Kissinger had worked hard and carefully to document beforehand—"No American stationed in Laos has ever been killed in ground combat operations."

This was Nixon's only reference to American casualties and other losses in Laos. He left it to his briefer to divulge, with a good deal of fumbling and correction, that in the neighborhood of 400 Americans (mostly airmen) had been killed or listed missing in six years, that some 400 aircraft had been lost, and that less than 50 civilians, later amended to 26, and then reestimated at less than 50, had been killed or listed as missing. The briefer repeatedly emphasized that no American, military or civilian, had been killed in ground combat, from which the reporters were invited to deduce that none had been or is engaged in ground combat. It turned out that at least one American, Captain Joseph Bush of Temple, Texas, who was stationed in Laos and serving with Laotian troops, had been killed in what any reasonable person would consider "ground combat operations." He was shot down by North Vietnamese commandoes on the night of February 11, 1969, while he was shooting at them and trying to repel an attack on the compound where he slept. A *Los Angeles Times* reporter with the Nixon press party in Miami told the White House staff on Saturday night, March 7, that the *Times* had a report to this effect from Don Schanche, a free-lancer who was in Laos at the time. The story appeared in the next morning's Sunday *Miami Herald* and a Nixon press spokesman dealt with it Sunday noon in these words: "The only comment that we would have would be that the President said on Friday there have been no Americans stationed in Laos killed in ground combat operations. A thorough check of the agency records showed that to be correct and still shows that to be correct."

Question: "Was the President aware of Captain Bush's death and the circumstances of it when he made that statement?"

Answer: "No."

Question: "Was the death of Captain Bush known to the official who prepared the statistics for the President?"

Answer: "As I said earlier, the records were thoroughly checked before the statement was made."

Question: "That would indicate he was?"

Answer: "No, that would indicate that he was not, that it was not [known to the official]."

So went, in Miami and afterward in Washington, the most inept performance that I have observed at the Nixon White House. Kissinger, who was in Miami with the President, was consulted before the unfortunate press officer who handled the initial inquiries dealt with them as he did. Press Secretary Ronald Ziegler said in Washington that it all was done "on White House authority," which had to mean if it meant anything that it was done on the President's authority. The later admission that Captain Bush had been awarded a posthumous Silver Star for gallantry, and that American military personnel in Laos draw combat pay—the Pentagon called it "hostile fire pay" and the White House followed suit—did not shake the official insistence that Nixon had been correct and remained correct in his statement that "No American stationed in Laos has ever been killed in ground combat action." The sole concession to common sense was the announcement that American casualties and aircraft losses in Laos would henceforth be disclosed when or soon after they occur—excepting casualties and losses from fighting on the Laos-Vietnam border.

It was a strange but instructive performance. It indicated that the President, Kissinger, and the others involved at the White House were so obsessed with their original determination to minimize the fact or possibility of American involvement in another ground war in Southeast Asia that they were incapable of perceiving the extent to which Mr. Nixon's credibility had been impaired in the effort to preserve it.

March 21, 1970

School
Statement

The President realized in July of 1969 that, at some point in some form, he would have to clarify and declare his policy on school desegregation. He was disturbed then by the confusions and conflicts of view within his Administration that preceded and followed a joint attempt by Attorney General John N. Mitchell and HEW Secretary Robert H. Finch to set forth the policy in a way that would at once appease Mr. Nixon's Southern white constituency and believably assert his adherence to the rightness of racial integration. That effort was a conspicuous and disgraceful failure. It encouraged Southern segregationists and further beclouded the President's already cloudy moral stance. It brought down upon the Administration the Supreme Court's unanimous declaration in October that deliberate segregation in the public schools must be ended now. And it brought Mr. Nixon to the dismal point, in February of 1970, of pretending to pledge "full support" to Senator John Stennis of Mississippi in his drive, successful for a time, to have Congress hold that deliberate (*de jure*) segregation, Southern style, and circumstantial (*de facto*) segregation everywhere must be treated by the federal government as if they were the same in origin, in effect, and in violation of law. This was not in fact the

President's view. He dreaded the possibility that it would become the Supreme Court's view, and his desire to do what he could to keep that from happening figured importantly in his decision, at mid-February, to prepare and issue the policy statement that appeared in his name on March 24.

One of five "Administration officials" who briefed the White House press corps when the statement was issued said that it was "rather uniquely the President's own work product . . . very much a personal document." Mr. Nixon put more of his own energy, time, and language into it than he had into any previous Presidential document, excepting only his November 3, 1969, Vietnam policy speech. He labored over successive drafts through the preceding fortnight, through the weekend of the postal crisis, and until 10 P.M. on the night before it was issued. But the work and views of many others, in and outside his official establishment, also went into it, and some account of what Mr. Nixon finally admitted to and excluded from his "personal document" should assist in the proper understanding of a policy statement that was intended by its ultimate author to defy conclusive understanding. "Watch for context," one of the President's official explainers admonished the press. "Watch for context, because I think you can develop a very misleading or mistaken set of assumptions from taking a paragraph or part of a paragraph out of its context and trying to work with it." When a reporter asked the same official why the President had not settled for the brief and reasonably explicit policy summary sandwiched at the middle of the 8000-word whole, the answer was that "if you had simply set out the principles on these two pages, the inevitable question would have been, 'Well, why didn't they do something about de facto segregation?' " This official had attended, on the preceding day, a meeting at which the question whether the President should deliver an abbreviated version on national television had been discussed. Raymond K. Price, Jr., a White House writer who did the basic drafting, had prepared two television drafts. They inevitably highlighted the policy summary and thrust into naked view the cautious negatives that largely characterize it and package for the segregationist South whatever comfort it may derive from the whole. The collective judgment of the assembled advisers was that "it comes out too negative," as one of them put it, and Mr. Nixon decided only on that day to forego TV.

The President had indicated in advance that he intended the

statement to be in major part a lawyer's brief, *his* brief, setting out
the law as he understood it to have been enacted by Congress and
declared by the courts. Attorney General Mitchell contributed substantially to the end product, though mostly by indirection. The
small task force that worked directly on the drafts heard from him
largely through the President via John Ehrlichman, the White
House assistant for domestic affairs. Mitchell took and pressed two
positions throughout the long preliminaries: get the Southern integration issue out of the way before this year's congressional and
state elections; and avoid like the plague any statement or action
that would encourage the Supreme Court to declare that *de facto*
school segregation is as illegal and unconstitutional as *de jure* segregation had long been known to be. Mitchell spoke through Nixon
in the sentence of the statement that said: "We should not provoke
any court to push a Constitutional principle beyond its ultimate
limit in order to compel compliance with the court's essential, but
more modest, mandate."

People who are unfamiliar with the Nixon operation might have
expected Commissioner of Education James E. Allen, Jr., a committed integrationist, to be consulted. He was, but only from the
maximum manageable distance and never in person by the President. Allen had succeeded, through a White House minion, in per-
suading Nixon to include in an earlier statement the flat assertion
that desegregation is vital to quality education. He had drafted, for
distribution in his own name, a strong statement to the same effect
when he learned in February that the President was working up his
own policy pronouncement. Allen submitted his draft to the White
House and hoped to the last that it would be adequately reflected.
It appeared only in a pallid acknowledgment that "under the ap-
propriate conditions, racial integration in the classroom can be a
significant factor in improving the quality of education for the dis-
advantaged."

The Administration officials who expounded for the President
made much of his prior consultation with Professor James Coleman, chief author of the famous "Coleman Report" on segregated
and integrated education. Coleman had one session of about 40
minutes with the President, found him to be an interested and per-
ceptive listener, and discussed the subject at greater length with
Ray Price and with Leonard Garment, a former Nixon law partner
and staff consultant on racial and civil rights problems. The profes-

sor's view that social and economic status and environment have more than race as such to do with educational results is reflected in the Nixon statement, parts of which Coleman reviewed with Price and Garment. Nixon assistants put it about afterward that Professor Coleman had been invited, and had agreed, to participate in supervising the studies of the problem that the President deems to be necessary before anyone can really know what effects integration does and doesn't have on the quality of education. This at the time was a considerable overstatement: the Professor had not been invited to participate, he had not promised to participate, and (as he said in a statement of his own) he strongly disagreed with those portions of the Nixon statement that indicated to him that the Administration was retreating from the effective prohibition of deliberate segregation in the South. He strongly agreed, he also said, with the portions that indicated to him that the Administration was committing substantial resources to "the implementation of school integration" everywhere.

The only new and positive step toward integration that the President committed himself to take, beyond the measures plainly required of him by Congress and the courts, was in his undertaking to enforce faculty desegregation everywhere. This was the last element of any importance added to the semi-final drafts. I gathered at the White House that it was introduced in a kind of trade-off for something else—probably, the official explanations seemed to suggest, for a more positive and general undertaking to move against de facto segregation than the issued statement contains.

Mr. Nixon promised to add $1.5 billion—half a billion in the next fiscal year, $1 billion in the following year—to the funds budgeted for educational purposes. This part of the statement has an odd history. It, too, was introduced at the very last, to beef up the substance of a notably insubstantial delineation of policy. Budget Director Robert Mayo heard of it only on the morning the statement appeared. The initial half billion has to come from previously budgeted funds, and Mr. Nixon told Republican congressional leaders that it would take him around three weeks to find the money. One of the budget bureau officials charged with finding it remarked to associates that he was "searching for funds in search of a program." The money may come and some of it probably will, from the little noticed cushion of $1.2 billion in uncommitted "contingency funds" that the President allowed himself in his fiscal

1971 budget. The indications are that the President will know where the money is to come from well before he knows what he is going to do with it. Three Nixon assistants—Ray Price, John Ehrlichman, and Leonard Garment—reacted with something close to hysteria to a *New York Times* headline suggesting that the money would be used principally to preserve *de facto* "segregated schools." They persuaded a *Times* reporter to take it back the next day.

April 4 & 11, 1970

X

Integrating
Friends

Watching Mr. Nixon's people in their first efforts to make decent sense of his school desegregation policy proved to be interesting and informative. Having declared his intention to enforce the laws and court decrees that he clearly has to enforce, and to keep the scope of enforceable law on the subject to the minimum that the courts will permit, the President left to Vice President Agnew, HEW Secretary Robert H. Finch, Attorney General John N. Mitchell, and numerous lesser subordinates the job of demonstrating just what he has in mind.

The initial demonstration was provided by Secretary Finch and J. Stanley Pottinger, the young California attorney who recently succeeded Leon Panetta, the fired director of HEW's Office for Civil Rights. That office is principally charged with enforcing Title VI of the Civil Rights Act of 1964, which forbids the federal government to support with federal funds any activity that discriminates against black and other minority Americans and, in particular, requires HEW to withhold federal money from any public school system that deliberately segregates black children and white children. The announced purpose of a press conference held by Finch and Pottinger was to explain how the Office for Civil

Rights proposes to enforce Title VI from now on, insofar as it
bears upon public schools. The true though unacknowledged purpose was to bury Title VI, insofar as it constitutes an immediate
sanction against deliberate segregation in the public schools.

Finch and Pottinger did their job with considerable skill. Pottinger said in a prepared statement that his office regards the Nixon
policy declaration of March 24 as "a clear mandate to bring into
compliance all school districts that discriminate." Finch said that
HEW hopes to double, from 1.2 million to 2.4 million, the number
of black children in integrated Southern schools by next September.
There was a lot of talk about monitoring the educational performance of Southern schools already in voluntary or enforced compliance with the requirements for integration. It was noted that "approximately 200 out of 4000 (Southern) school districts have not
submitted voluntary desegregation plans or become subject to court
ordered desegregation." But there was not a single reference, either
volunteered or in response to questions, to the law's requirement
that federal school funds be denied to holdout districts. In reading
the prepared statement, Pottinger omitted its remarkably mild assertion that "it is the policy of our office to *prompt* [my emphasis]
those schools which have been reluctant or unable to take their first
meaningful steps toward compliance." The fact, not mentioned at
the press conference, is that not one recommendation for the termination of federal funds for holdout districts has reached Secretary
Finch for his approval since July of 1969. Only two such recommendations are near the stage requiring his approval or disapproval,
and no more than ten others are creeping toward him through the
involved preliminary processes. Several factors, including a court
requirement for more positive proof of deliberate discrimination
than was necessary before last July, account for this state of affairs.
But the main factor is the Administration preference, first dictated
by Attorney General Mitchell and supported by Finch, for judicial
rather than executive enforcement of school desegregation.
    Finch made a great deal of his expressed hope that Congress will
quickly allow the Office for Civil Rights to increase its staff from
401 to 545 and come up by the summer with the first half billion of
the $1.5 billion that the President proposes to add in the next two

fiscal years to previously budgeted educational funds. An embar-
rassment in connection with the requested money was not mentioned. Mr. Nixon's assistants have said that he intends to spend
most of it to further desegregation rather than to improve the performance of "racially impacted" (meaning black) public schools.
The latter use of the money would imply a readiness to settle for if
not welcome the continuance of *de facto* segregation that the Administration is loath to confess. Nixon undertook to squeeze the
first half billion from other projects to which it had been allocated
in his 1971 budget, and the White House assistants looking for the
money have found it for him. Two statutes, the Civil Rights Act
and the Elementary and Secondary Education Act, provide ample
authority to support and encourage desegregation with the money.
But the use of federal funds for the benefit of schools in a condition
of "racial isolation"—the term now preferred to "segregation"—
may require new legislation, and how to ask Congress for it without
admitting a purpose that the Administration does not care to admit
was a problem yet to be solved.

Observant reporters at the Finch press conference noticed that
he was singularly restless toward the end of it. This was because he
was late for an unnanounced meeting of the new Cabinet Committee on Education at the White House. Vice President Agnew heads
the committee, and it is having its troubles. Its purpose is to make
the degree of further integration that the law and courts require Mr.
Nixon to impose upon the White South as palatable as possible to
that region, which is hard to do without making the purpose un-
comfortably clear. Agnew and others also were having trouble with
the committee's correct name. The President, who began by term-
ing it "a Cabinet-level working group," miscalled it the Cabinet
Committee on School Desegregation in his March 24 statement.
Robert C. Mardian, the California lawyer who has been HEW's
General Counsel and is now the committee's executive director,
sensed that a "Committee on School Desegregation" would not go
down too well with Mr. Nixon's white Southern constituency and
had a Presidential assistant announce, with emphasis, that it was to
be the Cabinet Committee on Education. When Mardian and
Agnew journeyed to Louisiana, on the first of a series of intended
endeavors to convince Southern officialdom that the Administration is doing only what it absolutely has to do in the way of enforc-

ing integration, and doing it with the utmost sympathy for the white South's problems, the Vice President persisted in referring to the Committee on School Desegregation.

Setting Agnew straight on this matter is the least of Robert Mardian's problems. He hopes, among other things, to recruit at least two respectable black Southerners, a lawyer and a public school official, for the committee staff on either a full-time or consultant basis. Fred Gray, a Montgomery attorney who is said at the White House to have represented black integrationists, agreed to visit Washington to discuss a possible association with the committee. A larger problem was just how to make known, to Deep South officialdom and to its community leaderships, black and white, the profound hope of the committee and of the Administration that influential Southerners will perceive the wisdom and desirability of voluntary rather than enforced integration of the remaining hardcore school districts and so (though nobody around Mr. Nixon says it) avoid the political harm that arbitrary measures would cause the Republican Party in the South. Mardian and the White House assistants with whom he is working first thought of firing off warm, explanatory letters to the Southern Governors. The absurdity of addressing such epistles to Lester Maddox of Georgia, John Bell Williams of Mississippi, and Claude Kirk of Florida dawned on the Nixon strategists, however, and they thereupon began casting about for other means of regional communication. Kirk, one of the lower South's two Republican governors, pointed up the difficulty when he tried to displace the Manatee County (Tampa) school board and thwart a federal district court order for complete and immediate integration of the local schools, with increased busing among other steps. Although the Justice Department dutifully intervened against Kirk, at the request of the offended court, the President's spokesmen at the White House did their best to detach Nixon from the affair. The court action that Kirk opposed is of the sweeping and arbitrary kind that Nixon deplored in his policy statement, and the Administration will be happier than it is likely to acknowledge if the end result is a Supreme Court finding that court orders of that sort go farther than the Constitution and the law require.

Clark Reed, the wealthy Mississippi bean farmer who is the Republican Party's state and regional chairman, provided one alternative channel of communication at a meeting that he arranged in

Washington with GOP chairmen and congressmen from Mississippi, Florida, Arkansas, and the two Carolinas. Jerris Leonard, the Assistant Attorney General for civil rights, said afterward that he had made it clear to the assembled Republicans that the Administration will have to enforce integration where it remains unenforced if they don't sell their holdout districts on the values of voluntary compliance. But it was Mardian, not Leonard, who dominated the closed meeting and came across to the conferees as the Nixon man to see about integration from now on. Clark Reed said after he got back to Mississippi that it was a useful and moderately comforting occasion. It convinced him and the other Southern Republicans that in Mardian, Leonard, and the President's other enforcers the South at last and at least has people that it can talk to and who will talk to it in a gentlemanly way. That it does.

April 18, 1970

"STOP BROODING, JOHN. WE'LL WHUP THEM DAMYANKEES YET."

X I

Rage at
the White House

San Clemente, California

The image of Richard Nixon that seems to be fixed in the minds of his closest servitors is so firm that they are slow to notice or acknowledge change in the man. Some among them say that, fifteen months after his inauguaration, the President is in all essentials of mien and behavior exactly as he was when he took office. They would say this even if it were pointed out to them that Nixon in the Presidency has never before behaved as he did on April 20, when he delivered his Vietnam speech from here, and as he had over the preceding weekend and throughout the period of unusual pressures that have borne upon him with increasing force since early March. In a burst of elation after watching the splashdown of the imperiled Apollo astronauts, he decided to fly 5000 miles across the Pacific in order to be seen in his brief act of honor to them. On equally sudden and unwonted impulse, he decided to fly back to Washington right after making his Vietnam broadcast instead of resting a second night, as he had planned, at his handsome home beside the sea. A reporter in the President's press party, mindful of Lyndon Johnson's addiction to abrupt movement and change of plan, was not altogether jesting when he said, "It will be funny, won't it, if the new Nixon turns out to be the old Johnson."

Some who serve Nixon, however, have noticed changes in him during the weeks of backfire from his inaccurate and unconvincing Laos statement on March 6; the strikes of postal workers and air controllers; the worsened situations that have confronted him in Laos, Cambodia, the Middle East; troubles with Congress over appropriations, inflation, defense, and racial policy; and, finally and most apparent in its effect upon him, the second rejection of a Southern nominee for the Supreme Court. The facade of imperturbability, the impression of cool efficiency and immunity to pressure that he and his assistants labored hard to construct and sustain during the prior months, have been cracked beyond repair.

At a meeting in his office in March, somebody remarked that the group should discuss what to do if Congress recessed for the Easter holiday without passing a delayed appropriation bill. Nixon startled his companions with the harsh ferocity of his response: "There will be no discussion! That decision has been made! They will have to come back!", meaning that he was determined to call the laggard legislators back in special session if need be. Toward the end of the mail crisis, when somebody suggested in the President's presence that the postal unions might not be as thoroughly committed to support of his revised postal reforms as he had been led to believe, and tried to make a joke of the uncertainty, Nixon said with chilling and astonishing intensity, "Let's stop this horsing around! It's time to start talking turkey!" The abrupt reactions, the manner and tone, were new to the Nixon Presidency, rare in occurrence but interesting in a man who had written years ago, in his *Six Crises,* of his self-discovered need to keep his impulses under rigid control and never, never to react to anything upon the heated instant. He liked to tell new associates, when he was training them for the 1968 campaign, that anger could be a useful trait in politics, useful if it was displayed in the right way at the right time. Display it, he said, only after the real anger had passed and then only when a controlled show of rage would serve an intended purpose.

The preferred story of the White House is that this is precisely what he did in that unforgettable two minutes on the afternoon of April 9, the day after the Senate had refused to confirm his nomination of G. Harrold Carswell for the Supreme Court. Then he stood before the White House press corps and television cameras and accused the 61 senators who had voted against one or both of his Southern choices of hypocrisy, vicious character assassination, sectional prejudice, and gross disregard of his, the President's, right and power of appointment. Contrived though his show of anger may have been, it left those of us who witnessed the performance in person frozen in our chairs for seconds after he whirled from the microphones and, with Attorney General Mitchell behind him, vanished from our view. The President's spoken remarks were derived from an even stronger and, in its language, more impassioned written statement that we were handed after he had returned to the Oval Office. The story of how that statement came into being does not invalidate the favored explanation that what we and televiewers saw was not real anger but a calculated simulation of anger. But it does demonstrate that Mr. Nixon acted on that occasion with a good deal less than his accustomed caution and control.

A general supposition has been that the statement and the spoken summary of it were talked out and thought out in the President's hitherto characteristic fashion the previous evening, when he took Mitchell and H. R. Haldeman, one of his chief assistants, with him for dinner aboard the yacht *Sequoia*. They discussed Carswell's defeat, the earlier defeat of Clement Haynsworth, and the President's continuing Supreme Court problem, along with other matters. But the President and his dinner guests had no idea then that Nixon would do what he did the following day. Near noon of that day he suddenly ordered preparatory work to be done, in a rush, on a statement or speech that was to deal with his Court problem in quite different and less abrasive terms. At around 2 P.M. Haldeman, speaking for Nixon, telephoned Patrick Buchanan, a White House staff writer, and instructed him to whip into shape, as soon as possible, a statement making the main points that Nixon later made. The version that had been ordered earlier went into limbo. At 3 P.M., when Mitchell joined Nixon in the President's office, Buchanan's draft was complete and in hand. Nixon discussed it with Mitchell and then dictated his own draft, the one that was published and from which he drew his televised outburst. The references to "hypocrisy," "vicious" and "malicious" maligning of Judges Carswell and Haynsworth, and some of the other similarly savage language were added by Nixon to the Buchanan draft. In the early evening, after filmed excerpts had appeared on television newscasts, Nixon took to the telephone and asked various assistants how they liked it. It was evident that he liked it very much indeed. His elation, his expressed delight with the whole performance, remind me of the euphoric state that he appeared to be in last summer after he let himself go with a militant speech on global policy at Colorado Springs and, soon afterward, with some unkind comments at a news conference upon the wisdom and abilities of former Defense Secretary Clark Clifford. Mr. Nixon's exuberance on April 9 carried over into the next day, the Friday of the Apollo splashdown. He still refused to have a TV set in his office, as he has since he had Lyndon Johnson's enormous array thrown out on Inaugural Day. But, in contrast to his restrained behavior during previous splashdowns, he watched this one in an adjoining office and clapped and did a little dance of joy when the Apollo three were safely down.

One of Mr. Nixon's purposes was to reaffirm his confidence in John Mitchell and to dispose of any notion that the President may or should have been impressed by the obvious flaws in the Attorney General's checks upon and judgments of Carswell and Haynsworth. There really should be no wonder at this. It is apparent from the public record, and from all that one hears on the subject at the Nixon White House, that the President simply refuses to believe that his closest associate and counsellor, Mr. Mitchell, erred in the slightest or that either Carswell or Haynsworth was proven to be unfit for the Supreme Court. If everything said and revealed about them before they were rejected had been known to Mr. Nixon when he nominated them, he would—I am convinced— have been as happy as he was without his later knowledge of them to submit their names to the Senate and, in so doing, to place his own powers of judgment on the line.

May 2, 1970

XII

Ins and Outs

Things that have never happened before at the Nixon White House kept happening in early May and the President's people kept saying that it didn't mean anything. Privately and in public, his assistants and spokesmen were edgy, more sensitive than they have previously appeared to be. James Keogh, chief of the White House writing staff, rebuked *The Washington Post* in a published letter for a minor misquotation of the President. Mr. Nixon, who has taken unabashed pleasure in the luxuries of the Presidency, directed the Secretary of Defense to sell two of the three Presidential yachts. Printed reports, including mine, that Mr. Nixon lately has acted at times on impulse, in alternating moods of anger and euphoria, were said on the highest authority short of the President himself to be inaccurate and outrageous. Mrs. Nixon's remark at a White House reception that her husband's trans-Pacific trip in honor of the Apollo astronauts had "wound him up" was not corrected, but the official line remained that nothing ever winds up Richard Nixon. While he pondered how and how far to act upon his declared view that a Communist takeover of Cambodia would endanger American forces in Vietnam and his hopes of reducing their role and numbers, he postponed three scheduled meetings of the National

Security Council, one after the other. It could not be denied that this was unprecedented, but it was said for him that he continues to rely, in the same old steady and cautious way, upon "the NSC process" in arriving at important decisions and pronouncements on foreign policy.

The variations from the previous norm were interesting because they occurred and because Nixon is Nixon. It was said on his behalf, and rightly, that if his predecessor, Lyndon Johnson, had reacted with no more discernible quivers than the incumbent President has in times of unusual pressure, Mr. Johnson would have been thought to be seriously off his feed. The assistant who made this point also advised me to skip the variations for a while and pay attention to some of the other things, more in keeping with the familiar Nixon, that have been going on recently at the White House. That was good advice, and I herewith follow it.

One of the nicer things was what almost happened to Richard D. Blumenthal, aged 24, late of Harvard, an independent Democrat of liberal mind who came to the White House staff last year with Counselor Daniel P. Moynihan. Mr. Nixon almost nominated him to be the director of Volunteers in Service to America (VISTA), and the President may do it yet. Dick Blumenthal is bright, handsome, attuned to his generation as very few others at the White House are. VISTA is a division of the Office of Economic Opportunity, and when former Congressman Donald Rumsfeld took over that agency last year Blumenthal was assigned to help him at the White House. VISTA, a kind of domestic Peace Corps which has some 5000 low-paid volunteers at rehabilitation work in ghettos and other depressed neighborhoods, was in need of a new director. William Ford, a Michigan Negro, didn't care for the atmosphere of Nixon's Washington and embarrassed the Administration by declining the appointment after it had been publicly offered him. Rumsfeld, impressed by Blumenthal's abilities, then went about suggesting him to the President in a way that tells a good deal about the Nixon White House. John D. Ehrlichman, the assistant for domestic affairs, asked some 15 other assistants of all ranks for their opinions of Blumenthal. Most of them approved, although a couple of them considered him too young and too liberal. Attorney General Mitchell, who had taped Blumenthal as a potentially dangerous radical, was won over in a personal talk with him. Only then was the idea mentioned to Mr. Nixon. He was said to be enthusiastic, recognizing as did others involved that the appointment would be a refreshing departure from the rather drab Nixon style. But Rumsfeld, complying with the cautious technique devised for Presidential choices, did not then recommend the Blumenthal appointment in a way that would require final approval. Blumenthal was unconventionally young, he had no administrative experience, and the anti-poverty agency was in trouble with Congress. So Blumenthal was instructed to clear himself with certain doubtful Senators who would have to confirm the nomination. This he did. Then another, at least temporarily decisive, obstacle was discovered. Blumenthal had an occupational deferment from the draft, the President was about to recommend the abolition of all such deferments, and Rumsfeld barred them by executive order in his own agency. Blumenthal gave up and enlisted in the Marine Corps Reserve for a six-months training period. The word at the White House and at OEO is that he has a standing invitation to come back and take the VISTA directorship. That was not his understanding when he left and it still is not the impression of some of his friends in Washington. Their impression was and is that "the climate wasn't right" for such an appointment and they will be pleasantly surprised if Rumsfeld and Nixon prove them wrong.

Things also have been happening to Harry Dent of South Carolina, one of the President's four Special Counsels and, by designation last year, Mr. Nixon's political coordinator. Murray M. Chotiner of California, a Nixon friend and associate from the President's early years in politics, moved in with Dent and with the co-equal status of Special Counsel in early 1970. Chotiner said that he has the responsibility for servicing the needs of congressmen, Republican politicians, and state and county officials in 31 states and that Harry Dent has similar responsibilities in 19 states, mostly in the South. This arithmetic could suggest that Harry Dent has been substantially downgraded. Both Dent and Chotiner say in different ways that this is not the fact. "I'm still responsible for all political liaison," Dent says. "Murray doesn't work totally in this area, and when he does he coordinates with me. I still have the total responsibility for the whole thing." Chotiner speaks of his 31 states as though they were pretty much his own, but he agrees that he keeps in touch with Dent and he says for the record, "I have seen and observed nothing to indicate any loss of footing in any manner whatsoever so far as Harry Dent is concerned." Chotiner also says that he had practically nothing to do with the frantic White House efforts to get Judge G. Harrold Carswell confirmed for the Supreme Court, and nothing whatever to do with the embarrassing imbroglio that attended Judge Carswell's resignation from the Fifth Circuit Court of Appeals and candidacy for the Republican nomination for Senator from Florida. "Florida," Chotiner says with great contentment "is one of Harry's states."

Another Special Counsel who has had his troubles is Clark Mollenhoff, a lawyer and investigative reporter who was installed at the White House last fall and charged with preserving the Nixon Administration from preventable sin. Mollenhoff, an enthusiastic talker with a high and well-earned opinion of himself, volunteered to a group of reporters the interesting information that he was authorized by the President to call for and inspect the tax returns of anybody in the United States. Senator Albert Gore of Tennessee and other legislators called in Treasury officials to explain and, if they could, justify what seemed to them to be an alarming grant of authority to a White House prober. What most disturbed them and many of Molenhoff's former colleagues in journalism was the picture of him as a totally independent operator, under no check whatever except the little that might be provided by a busy President. The facts are that Mollenhoff reports to the President and gets his directions from the President through Mr. Nixon's administrative chief, H. R. Haldeman, and that Haldeman keeps track of what Mollenhoff is doing at all times. Why the White House spokesmen didn't still the Mollenhoff storm by saying as much is something of a mystery. "You mean," one of Haldeman's senior associates said when this was suggested, "that Bob Haldeman would be considered more dependable than Clark Mollenhoff?" That may be so, but it is not the point. The point is that senators and citizens generally would prefer to believe that there is some check upon the investigative powers of a Presidential assistant charged with Mollenhoff's duties. But it's the kind of point that is overlooked more often than one might suppose at the cautious and orderly Nixon White House.

May 9, 1970

Soon after the foregoing report appeared, Mollenhoff resigned and Dick Blumenthal decided that he didn't want any job with the Nixon Administration. Murray Chotiner left the White House staff but did not leave Mr. Nixon's political service in early 1971.

"THERE'S GOT TO BE SOME OTHER WAY OUT OF IT..."

XIII

The Road
to Madness

Retracing the President's road to the current madness in Cambodia is a painful exercise for one who has been persuaded and has reported, as I have been reporting since the summer of 1969, that Mr. Nixon had a better understanding of the nature of the Vietnam war and was working toward a saner solution of the Vietnam problem than he thought it wise or possible to indicate in public. I have written in effect that he really understood that, as he said so recently as April 20, "A political settlement is the heart of the matter." And I have written that he was prepared to pay any price in the form of concession to the Vietnam Communists that a political settlement required, if only they would heed his many public and private signals to that effect and begin to bargain seriously with the American negotiators in Paris.

The saddest thing to be said of Mr. Nixon in the light of the Cambodia decision is that all of this was true and that in terms of his ultimate hopes and intentions it is still true. It is sad because he has made the truth unbelievable with his deliberate extension of the war from South Vietnam into neutral Cambodia and with the wild and irresponsible rhetoric in which he clothed the announcement of his act on April 30. His talk in that announcement of the "intolerable" attitude of an enemy that has presumed to ignore the warnings of "the richest and strongest nation in the history of the world," and his professed refusal to accept "a peace of humiliation" at "the cost of seeing America become a second-rate power," obscured and seemed to negate the passage in which he also said: "The time came long ago to end this war through peaceful negotiations. We stand ready for those negotiations. We have made major efforts, many of which must remain secret. All the offers and approaches made previously remain on the conference table whenever Hanoi is ready to negotiate seriously."

The offers and approaches and the policy that they reflected date back to May 14, 1969, when Mr. Nixon renounced "a purely military solution" in Vietnam and moved toward the course of gradual troop withdrawal. Then and in the months that followed, he said and reiterated that every issue involved in the Vietnam war was negotiable except "the opportunity for the South Vietnamese people to determine their own future." That condition could be and was interpreted as a cover for rigid and self-defeating support of the Thieu regime in Saigon, but it was qualified in open and secret ways that were intended to draw Hanoi and the Vietcong into practical negotiation. The Hanoi government was offered a place on an international commission that would supervise postwar elections in South Vietnam. The Vietcong was offered a right to contest the elections "as an organized force" and thus, by clear implication, any role that it might win politically in any elected postwar government. The suggestion that much broader concessions were possible, given serious negotiation, was implicit in the public statements of these offers and it was made explicit in private assurances conveyed to Hanoi. The supporting policy of "Vietnamization," meaning the training and equipment of the South Vietnamese military to take over ground combat as American troop levels were reduced, was intended to convince Hanoi and the Vietcong leadership that they confronted a genuine choice between a negotiated settlement, profitable to them, and indefinite warfare at a cost they could not forever afford.

Mr. Nixon and the principal co-architect of the total policy, his
adviser Henry Kissinger, believed through the summer and well
into the fall of 1969 that it was going to work. They expected it to
bring about productive negotiation in Paris and a settlement that
would end the war on terms short of acknowledged defeat and humiliation for the United States. Their expectations faded into
hopes, and the hopes began to fade toward despair, in the Septem-
ber-October period. Mr. Nixon's major policy statement on November 3 reflected the change, but the promise to Hanoi of substantial concessions if only it would enter serious negotiation was
still implicit and continued to be emphasized in private explanations of the policy at the White House. That statement, like the
ones that preceded and followed it, did not have the intended effect
upon Hanoi. But its impact at home had a profound and, as we are
seeing now, a fateful effect upon Mr. Nixon. The public support
that his November 3 speech won for him persuaded the President
that getting out of the war was not as imperative as he had thought
it was. The effect was first apparent on December 15 when he
quoted a statement equating "a just peace" with "maintaining an
independent, non-Communist South Vietnam" and said that it was
"in line with my own attitude." By pledging himself to accept any
outcome of elections in South Vietnam, including if need be a
Communist or coalition government, Mr. Nixon had previously
and deliberately, in the interest of encouraging negotiation, renounced the hitherto basic American premise that the preservation
of a "non-Communist South Vietnam" was essential to American
security. The shift in tone, hardly noticed at the time, presaged his
plunge into the rhetoric of April 30, with its neurotic theme that
"the world's most powerful nation" would be acting "like a pitiful,
helpless giant" if it tolerated the presence and threat of perhaps
40,000 Communist troops along South Vietnam's Cambodian borders.

It is being said at the White House now, with no sense of confession or error, that the President did not estimate the threat from
Cambodia in that way only 10 days before he ordered American
troops into Cambodia. In his broadcast speech of April 20, announcing his intention to reduce American forces in Vietnam by
150,000 within 12 months, he warned Hanoi that he would "take

strong and effective measures" if it responded to the American
withdrawal with "increased military action in Vietnam, in Cambodia, or in Laos." But I know of no reason to disbelieve the flat
assertions of his principal staff advisers that he did not then consider the North Vietnamese and Vietcong presence and activities
in Cambodia to require the measures that he took on April 30.

The offered explanation is ludicrous in its bald insufficiency. It
is, of course, that the overthrow of Prince Sihanouk's neutral government by rightist General Lon Nol and his clique and the subsequent movement of North Vietnamese and Vietcong Communists
upon the capital at Pnompenh threatened to turn the whole of
Cambodia into an enemy redoubt for use against the American
forces in South Vietnam. Prince Sihanouk was overthrown in his
absence on March 19. The consequent threat to Pnompenh and
Communist advances in the Cambodian countryside had been evident for more than two weeks when Mr. Nixon spoke on April 20.
His very special spokesman, produced as is usual on such occasions, said that the Communist forces known to be in action within
Cambodia against Cambodian forces totaled no more than 5000
troops, operating in units of a few hundred. Defense Secretary
Melvin Laird said in another special press briefing at the Pentagon
that the movement of Communist supplies from North Vietnamese
"sanctuaries" in Cambodia into the bordering Delta and Saigon
areas of South Vietnam had dropped "to zero" in the weeks just
preceding the American attacks upon those sanctuaries. His remark was one of the many odd and inherently contradictory justifications of the American ground attacks and of the resumed bombing of North Vietnam border targets that characterized the official
performance in the aftermath of the President's action. It was all
too believable that the vaunted "Vietnamization" process was
threatened with failure and required at least another six months of
maximum American support and protection. This claim, amount-
ing as it did to an unintended confession that the Nixon policy was
in danger of collapse, was just about the only thing said in behalf of
his action that was wholly believable.

What, then, had happened? One thing that had happened beyond
dispute (though it was disputed) was a visible change in Mr.
Nixon's mode of behavior. He had been tiring himself, to an extent
and in ways that he for years had consciously schooled himself not
to do. He himself said, for example, that he was up until 5 A.M. on

April 30, writing and rewriting the speech that he delivered that night after briefing congressional leaders for 45 minutes. But this, in my guess, was only a symptom of the fundamental happening that explained, better than all of his and his spokemen's words, the decision to order the invasion that was "not an invasion of Cambodia." Mr. Nixon, again in my guess, had been brought to recognize the failure, actual in part and impending in part, of his entire Vietnam policy—negotiation, Vietnamization and all—and the recognition was more than he could bear with his usual quietude.

May 16, 1970

"BUT I <u>AM</u> TUNED IN TO YOUTH—JULIE, AND DAVID, AND TRICIA..."

XIV

On the Phone

Just being around the White House in mid-May, as close (which isn't very close) as reporters are allowed to get to the real doings there, has been educational. It has been a time for watching the President under stress, for observing the effect of his performance upon some of the people who work for him and who, like the reporters, learn or at least come to realize things about his personality and his leadership and the processes of national decision that were hidden or dimly perceived at best during the first 15 months of the Nixon Presidency.

The staff habit of denying, for instance, that Mr. Nixon ever loses his cool, tires himself beyond the limits of prudence, and says and does things in those circumstances that he later regrets suddenly went out of fashion. It was said for him last week, not as in the past that he never has a sleepless night, but that it would be a gross and damaging exaggeration to say that he has had a whole string of them since this time of heightening and unceasing pressures upon him began in early March. Mr. Nixon made the former claim impossible with his performance on the night of his May 9 press conference and through the dawn and morning of the following day, the Saturday of the rally of antiwar students and other protesters in Washington. A change had occurred, an act of recognition and understanding had taken place at the White House, when it could be said as I heard it said there about that Saturday, "It wouldn't have been a good day for something bad to happen, would it?"

After the press conference, which I thought the President handled with impressive skill, he wanted to talk to people and he wanted to be as he had been through most of the preceding day—alone. The telephone enabled him to have it both ways, and he made ample and revealing use of an instrument to which, it turns out, he is as devoted as Lyndon Johnson was. First in his Oval Office in the West Wing of the White House, and then in the adjoining Mansion, he talked and talked and talked with people who called him and whom he called. Mrs. Nixon, his two daughters and his son-in-law, David Eisenhower, were away for the night at Camp David in Maryland. He was full of the press conference, of what he took to be his successful effort to be at once firm and conciliatory. He said that the Cambodian decision had been his alone, it was *right,* and even the protesters gathering in their thousands that night would come to see that it was, although of course they would never admit it. He talked, too, of his need to be understood and of the troubling failure and refusal of so many people to understand him and the nature of the Presidency. He told some of his callers to study, to think about, the press conference answer in which he had spoken of senators and others who "have the luxury of criticism" and had said of himself, "I don't have that luxury." He had been trying, he said, to get across what it meant to have the final and total responsibility for the decisions a President has to make, not just about Vietnam and Cambodia but about the whole range of our problems.

He spoke to others of the number and complexity of those problems, of his own problem of communicating with all of the segments of a divided society in ways that would not alienate one segment while pleasing others. He knew better than his critics, he said, how deep and dangerous the divisions were. What could he do, what could he say, to manage and heal and lessen the divisions? He spoke in particular of his liberal critics. When would they understand, would they ever understand, that he was more liberal than many of them were? His Quaker forebears on his mother's side, the Milhouses, had risked their lives before the Civil War with the un-

dergroud railroad of that day, bringing black slaves from the
South to freedom in Indiana. How, with such an ancestry, could he
be the blind conservative that so many liberals seemed to think he
was? What—again—could he do, what could he say that he hadn't
been doing and saying to convince them, the Negroes and black-
hating whites, the antiwar students and the blue-collar people who
hated *them* (he mentioned the construction workers on pro-war
rampage in New York City), that he sympathized with their frus-
trations and understood the difficulties that different kinds of
Americans have in living with and adjusting to each other.

At 1:30 A.M. he rang up Nancy Dickerson of NBC, who with a
question at the press conference had given him the first of two
chances to say at once that he wanted to quiet the more abusive
rhetoric of his Administration and that he was not about to muzzle
Vice President Agnew or any other official. Miss Dickerson recalled
to him that he had said he would be glad to meet some of the student
demonstrators in person if it could be arranged and she urged him
to do it. "Why, I really love those kids," he said. "I've told Haldeman and Ehrlichman"—H. R. Haldeman and John D. Ehrlichman,
his chief domestic assistants—"to bring them in. I want to see them
all." It seemed to her that the President was pleading to be believed, to be understood by her and others as he understood himself. At 3:30, still up and at it, he telephoned Helen Thomas, one
of United Press International's White House reporters. He had
closed the press conference with a moment of tribute to Merriman
Smith, a UPI reporter who had covered the White House since
1934 and had shot himself in April. The President was rambling a
little by that hour, his tiredness came over the telephone to Miss
Thomas, but so did his affection for "Smitty" and his desire that
she understand that his gesture the night before had come from the
heart.

The President said later that he went to bed for an hour or so,
didn't sleep well, and got up and telephoned Manolo Sanchez.
Manolo, Mr. Nixon's Cuban-American valet, is also a friend and
companion, a lively and witty and loyal servant with whom Mr.
Nixon seems to be comfortable in much the way that he is comfortable with C. G. (Bebe) Rebozo, the Florida neighbor and busi-
nessman who is often with the President and his family in Miami,

in Washington, in California. Sanchez and his wife live at the Mansion, on the floor above the Nixon quarters. What happened after Manolo was awakened and summoned made national and now familiar news: the President and Manolo driving with a few "petrified" Secret Service men to the Lincoln Memorial at 5 A.M., the President rousing and talking, trying "to relate," with a few sleepy student demonstrators; then on to the Capitol, a hurried tour of the Rotunda and the House chamber; and finally, joined by five frantically alerted staff assistants, a breakfast of eggs and hash—his first in five years, the President later said—at the Mayflower Hotel. Mr. Nixon insisted on telling it all for himself, after his return to the White House at 7:37, and the memorable thing about his appealing and happy account is that it consisted almost entirely of what he said to the students and almost nothing of what they said to him. The few among them who were found and interviewed afterward indicated that they were dazed, baffled, as if caught in a dream that—one of them said—should never have happened. It was an unkind reaction, not the effect that the President obviously sought, but other adults who have tried "to relate" with youngsters of the kind encountered at the Lincoln Memorial must sympathize with Mr. Nixon and award him a plus for trying.

Through the day of demonstrations that followed, some of the President's assistants received and listened to and talked with several hundred students and faculty members who were invited in from the guarded streets. Mr. Nixon saw none of them—it was, as he said, difficult to arrange with discretion and without seeming to exploit them. He worked awhile in the Oval Office and walked out of the West Wing for a chat with an Army detail concealed, just in case, in the basement of the adjoining Executive Office Building. Around one o'clock he took a pre-luncheon nap and then worked as usual through the afternoon. He must have heard, though nothing was said about his hearing, the hugely amplified sound rolling from the Ellipse, south of the White House, where somewhere between 60,000 and 100,000 protesters were assembled, suffering gladly in the hot sun and visibly bored with the expectable platform rhetoric except when, as at one unplanned moment, a speaker yelled through the loudspeakers and over TV: FUCK RICHARD NIXON! That was not the mood, or anyhow the expressed mood, of the students who were invited to come in and talk with Nixon aides. They were said to have been mostly attentive, deeply concerned with Cambodia and with much else that they thought wrong with American society and with the Administration, and more pleased than a good many of them wanted to admit with this access to people who might pass along their views to the President. I never could get it confirmed that the memorandum accounts of the student sessions prepared by the staff hosts actually reached the President; it was said only that the essence of them did in one form or another. But it was clear enough that Mr. Nixon and his principal assistants had come alive to a need for communication and a gap in their communication with the more restless elements in divided America that he and most of the men who serve him had been disastrously slow to recognize.

All the while, of course, the Cambodian invasion proceeded and was declared to be "an enormous success" by the President's spokesmen. The show of early withdrawal of some of the American troops from Cambodian territory, the deluge of statistics on captured munitions and destroyed enemy bunker complexes (not including the North Vietnamese-Vietcong "headquarters" that the President had been so confident of finding), served to muffle the anxieties that Mr. Nixon had aroused and to postpone, though surely not for long, the realization that another country has in fact been brought into the theater of the Vietnam war and into the area of Southeast Asia requiring American defense. Mr. Nixon, having indulged his need to explain himself and to make himself understood, has in prospect the larger job of explaining what he has done in Asia and of making that understood in the way he wants it to be. He has not, one could predict, had his last sleepless night.

May 23, 1970

XV

Cabinet Capers

Reporters at the White House were mildly puzzled in mid-May when they were told that George Romney, the Secretary of Housing and Urban Development, had regaled a Cabinet meeting that day with an account of his visit to a new and experimental federal information center in Philadelphia. The center is one of several where citizens are supposed to be able to find out whatever they want to know about government services and agencies. It was puzzling because Romney and Counselor Daniel P. Moynihan, the President's urban specialist, had visited the Philadelphia center weeks before and had already favored the press with a detailed and rather dull account of their findings that the center was a success. Why take up the President's and the Cabinet's time at that late date with the same report?

The answer tends to confirm an impression that the Cabinet as an institution, a body that has to be called into session at decent intervals in respect for tradition and for the egos of its members, has become something of a nuisance to modern Presidents. Alexander P. Butterfield, a deputy assistant to the President who has been functioning as the "Cabinet coordinator" since November of 1969, had been unable to fill the agenda for that day's meeting. He customarily schedules three items for Cabinet discussion, plus a fourth that is always labeled "Remarks of the President" on a memorandum distributed in advance to Cabinet members. Butterfield shops around among department heads for matters thought to be worth discussion and submits their suggestions to the President, who usually approves whatever is offered him but sometimes strikes out one or more items and substitutes his own. Nobody came up with a third suggestion for the meeting in question, Butterfield put out an SOS for help and Romney and Moynihan, both of whom are avid talkers, gladly filled the gap.

Butterfield acquired the chore of Cabinet coordinator by default. Another deputy assistant, John C. Whitaker, was designated Cabinet Secretary when Mr. Nixon took office with the usual affirmations that he expected to make his Cabinet a viable and valued forum for counsel and discussion at the peak of federal power. Whitaker, in addition to setting up meeting schedules and acting as the President's liaison man with Cabinet members, found himself devoting much of his time to the needs and demands of Cabinet wives. They looked to him for such things as special White House tours for their out-of-town guests and access to the Presidential yacht *Sequoia* for their husbands' more-or-less official dinners. A discreet young man, not given to complaint, Whitaker was said to have been pleased and relieved when the President took him along on the Nixon tour of Asia. The aftermath details from that trip continued to occupy him, somebody had to attend to Cabinet matters, and the task fell to Butterfield. He was then and still is one of the senior deputies to H. R. Haldeman, the administrative chief of the White House staff.

The formal abandonment of the title of Cabinet Secretary and Butterfield's formal designation as Cabinet coordinator accompanied a major rearrangement, in late 1969, of the responsibilities shared by Haldeman and John D. Ehrlichman, who was then entitled the Assistant for Domestic Affairs. Whitaker was transferred from Haldeman's to Ehrlichman's larger and still expanding staff at about the same time that several other changes, petty but symptomatic of the Nixon establishment's preoccupation with structure, were occurring. Haldeman relinquished to Butterfield a small office directly adjoining the President's Oval Office, along with the physical handling and delivery to Mr. Nixon of documents prepared for him, and moved down the West Wing hall to a large corner office

which until then had been reserved for but seldom used by Vice
President Agnew. Dwight Chapin, another Haldeman staffer who
schedules the President's visitors and performs innumerable personal services, moved from a corridor desk into an office of his
own, across the hall from Butterfield's, and delegated to a young
assistant named Stephen Bull the usher's task of seeing visitors in
and out of the Oval Office. Both Haldeman and Chapin, it is said,
have more time than they had before these changes for thinking
about what they should do for the President and are not so bur-
dened with the mean details of doing it.

    Ehrlichman, acknowledged to be the chief assistant for purposes
of domestic policy formulation and management, went to elaborate
lengths to insure adequate liaison and cooperation with the statutory Cabinet members and the departments they head. Haldeman's
man, Butterfield, confines himself to arrangements for the infre-
quent Cabinet meetings and leaves all else, including the wants of
Cabinet wives, to six Ehrlichman assistants who deal with the domestic departments and agencies. The assistant assigned to Agriculture, Interior, and some bureaus of the Commerce Department
is the former Cabinet Secretary, John Whitaker. One of his Secretaries is Walter Hickel of Interior, who projected himself into national view on May 7 in the unlikely role of the Cabinet's leading
liberal and advocate of a degree of concern for the nation's rebel-
lious youth that the Administration had not displayed up to then.
    Hickel accomplished this with a letter to the President, the one
in which he suggested that Vice President Agnew be ordered to
moderate his divisive rhetoric and that Mr. Nixon, among other
things, "consider meeting on an individual and conversational basis
with members of your Cabinet." Hickel's staff leaked the letter the
day it was written to three newspapers, before it had reached the
President, and also confided to the press that Hickel had enjoyed
only two private meetings with the President in 15 months. Everything said in the letter needed saying; it helped bring into the open
discontents at Cabinet level with Nixon policies varying from Vietnam and Cambodia to counter-inflationary measures and the Administration's grievous lack of response to domestic unrest, and
Secretary Hickel deserved the accolades that he immediately received and invited for himself on national television. But the epi-

sode had its odd aspects, unnoticed in the general acclaim for a Cabinet rebel, and they suggest that Mr. Hickel chose his time and occasion with care.

His televised account (on the CBS Mike Wallace show), plus the tidbit about the two private meetings, left the impression that a Cabinet member with urgent need of consultation with the President was shut off from Mr. Nixon, not only then but all the time, by the White House establishment. What is really shown is that the White House establishment is singularly inept at setting forth facts that serve its President's cause and that, in this instance, Secretary Hickel was in no mood to supply them himself. He knows, as does every other department head and Cabinet member, that within reason he can see the President privately whenever he needs to. The reason Mr. Hickel had seen the President alone only twice in 15 months was that he had asked for only two meetings in that time. The day that he chose to demand a third meeting in private was Tuesday, May 5, when the President was involved for more than five hours with House and Senate committeemen, explaining and defending the Cambodian decision, and in addition was awakening—without Secretary Hickel's proffered assistance—to the significance and impact of the killing of four Kent State University students by Ohio National Guardsmen on the previous Monday afternoon. Told that Mr. Nixon was too busy to see him, Hickel asked his White House intermediary, the unfortunate Whitaker, to set up a meeting or telephone talk with Ehrlichman. It so happened— and prying this fact out of the White House staff was like extracting eye-teeth—that Ehrlichman had departed on the afternoon of the Kent State killings for Charlottesville, Virginia, where he addressed a seminar of federal officials assembled there from all over the country, and remained well into the Tuesday. Given five or ten minutes of talk by telephone or in person with Ehrlichman, Hickel later said, he probably would not have written the letter. Whitaker told Hickel that it was impossible to get Ehrlichman on the telephone—an extraordinary claim, since White House assistants are supposed never to be out of reach of the telephone. As for the demanded meeting with Mr. Nixon, the Secretary's account indicates that he dealt only with John Whitaker although he knew, as he said on television, that Haldeman and Chapin are the ones to see about seeing the President.

Cabinet members often rely upon their assigned liaison man, in this instance Whitaker, to make the requested arrangement with Haldeman or Chapin, but it seems odd that Secretary Hickel, given the state of agitation and insistence in which he says he was, did not appeal directly and for himself to one of the two keepers of the Nixon door. On the next day, Wednesday, the President appeared from his published schedule to be less pressed than he had been on Tuesday. But Hickel was occupied in polishing the final draft of his letter that morning, somebody on his staff was busy preparing to leak it, and nothing happened to impede one of the more interesting episodes of the Nixon Presidency.

May 30, 1970

———

A White House assistant had the foregoing account photocopied, hugely enlarged, and presented to Mr. Hickel with the assistant's compliments.

XVI

Paying
for Integration

It is a pleasure to report that Mr. Nixon has come up with something good. His message of May 21 on public school desegregation, the accompanying Emergency School Aid Act of 1970, and his request for $1.5 billion in extra money over the next two years to help with the elimination and, where that is impossible, the diminution of racial separation in the schools are blows for justice and decency in a field where the President and his Administration have not previously been distinguished for either quality. This could not be said with confidence if the President's words on the subject were all that there is to go by. But there is more, in the form of real action by the principal agencies of federal enforcement, the Department of Justice and the Office for Civil Rights in the Department of Health, Education, and Welfare. Beyond question, they are moving with hitherto missing vigor against the remnants of deliberate (*de jure*) segregation in the South and are trying to come to grips with the more difficult problems of circumstantial (*de*

facto) racial separation and discrimination in public schools elsewhere.

Manifestly, in view of the Administration's past record of equivocation and disgraceful catering to racial prejudices in its dealings
with the problems of segregation and integration in the public
schools, some important changes must have occurred if the foregoing judgment is correct. There have indeed been changes, outside of
and within the Administration, and a review of them is necessary if
the new stance is to be understood. Virtue in this matter has been
forced upon the Administration, a fact that may be stated and kept
in mind without denying Mr. Nixon and his concerned subordinates all credit for at last recognizing both the necessity and the
potential political rewards of doing what the law, the courts, and
even the dimmest understanding of the national good require them
to do.

The decisive change occurred in October 1969 when the Supreme Court ruled, after 15 years of putting up with persisting
segregation in Southern schools, that what remained of it must be
ended "at once." That decision, expanded in subsequent court findings to require an end to Southern school segregation by the fall of
1970 at the latest, set in train a series of revised calculations within
the Administration that is still in process. Attorney General John
N. Mitchell, who had brought the October decision upon himself
and the President with a cynical and foolish request that the Supreme Court permit a further delay in the integration of Mississippi
schools, was impelled in indirect consequence of it to abandon the
position that had governed the Administration's approach. This
position was that executive enforcement of school integration, by
depriving segregated schools of federal funds as required by Title
VI of the Civil Rights Act, was both unnecessary and politically silly.
Why continue to anger and alienate white Southerners, he argued,
when the onus for enforcement could be shifted to the courts by
initiating suits instead of cutting off federal money from districts
that, once under court order, would get their federal funds whether
or not their desegregation plans satisfied HEW? The last thing he
expected was the Supreme Court's October ruling in circumstances
that his own lawyers had brought about.

The result was that the political profit from judicial rather than
executive action vanished. Mr. Mitchell's restraining hand was
lifted from HEW's Office for Civil Rights, and it and his depart-

ment's civil rights division are again permitted to work in effective concert, with a combination of court and administrative action. HEW Secretary Robert H. Finch was able to say in good conscience, as he did on May 18, that "the Administration is committed unequivocally to the enforcement of Title VI," and to resume the termination of federal funds for holdout school districts.

The Administration was still adjusting to the consequences of the Supreme Court's October decision when, in February, Mr. Nixon put Vice President Agnew at the head of what has since come to be called the Cabinet Committee on School Desegregation. One of the ironies of the Nixon time is the fact that this outfit, initially intended to make the final and unavoidable phase of school integration as palatable as possible to Southern segregationists, became the vehicle for producing the President's May 21 message and legislation. The message was drafted by the White House staff, principally by Special Consultant Leonard Garment and one of Mr. Nixon's more enlightened writers, Raymond K. Price, Jr., and the legislation was prepared in the main at HEW. But the program had to be thrashed out within the Cabinet committee before the President would accept it, and that required an improbable consensus among such figures as Attorney General Mitchell, Postmaster General Winton Blount, and Agnew on the one hand, and Secretaries Finch and George Shultz, the committee's vice chairman and active head, on the other.

The basis for consensus, the factor that made it possible, is perfectly clear, although it has been obscured by the subsequent claim, natural enough in the circumstances, that a fundamental affinity for social decency on the part of the President and his advisers accounts for it. The determining fact is that the President, the Cabinet committee, and the various assistants and consultants who had a hand in the outcome found themselves in a situation where decency was bound to pay off. The South's remaining segregated schools had to desegregate, the Supreme Court and the lower federal courts had made further delay impossible, and the Administration had no practicable choice but to make the process as acceptable and rewarding as it could. Most of the requested $1.5 billion in special funds—$500 million in the next fiscal year, $1 billion in fiscal 1972—is earmarked, Congress willing, for Southern school districts that are integrating now or have integrated in the past two years. Token amounts, so small proportionately that HEW and White House spokesmen refused to specify them, may also go to urban and non-Southern districts with predominantly black and other minority school student bodies. But the chief and declared objective is to reward while helping the white South in its enforced surrender to integration.

Mr. Nixon exaggerated when he said in his May 21 message that "more than 500 Northern districts are under review or likely soon to be under review for possible violations of Title VI." HEW's Office for Civil Rights can cite at the most 38 to 40 "active cases" of suspected discrimination in non-Southern school districts, but it and the Justice Department are moving where they find actionable evidence of deliberate segregation outside the South. Stanley Pottinger, the young Californian who replaced the fired Leon Panetta as head of OCR, notified school districts with substantial numbers of Puerto Rican, Mexican-American, and other non-English speaking students that they will lose their federal funds unless they end forthwith practices that penalize such children for their lack of English. Some of the extra money requested by Mr. Nixon may go to such districts for hiring bilingual teachers and consultants, and more is intended for school systems that undertake either to diminish *de facto* black-white segregation or to ameliorate the educational harm done by racial isolation arising from community housing patterns. A small staff of consultants, among them Professor James Coleman of Johns Hopkins University, is working with the Agnew committee to formulate valid criteria for the granting and use of all the new money, whether among the primary Southern beneficiaries or among school districts elsewhere that qualify for supplementary aid. The program took a month longer to fashion than Mr. Nixon had expected when he ordered its preparation on March 24, and one of the reasons for delay was that the men who put it together realized as they went along that they were evolving something more than the "emergency" approach called for by the President. Out of the sordid beginnings of this Administration's handling of the racial aspects of public education, emerged a more enlightened attitude than anyone had a right to expect. Senator Walter Mondale of Minnesota, chairman of a select committee on equal educational opportunity, was justified in saying that the new Nixon program "is certainly not sufficient to repair the damage done to the cause of integrated education over the past 16 months." But the damage done has been acknowledged, indirectly, and the need to repair it has been recognized.

June 6, 1970

———

The 91st Congress appropriated only $75 million and postponed action on the remainder of the requested $1.5 billion until 1971. Formal segregation all but vanished from the South's public schools, but blatant discrimination persisted in many nominally "desegregated" school systems.

"OKAY, SPIRO, YOU WERE GREAT. NOW GET BACK HERE."

XVII

Blessed
Assurance

San Clemente, California

One of the hymns that the crowd in the University of Tennessee football stadium at Knoxville sang for God and the President on the night of May 28 was *Blessed Assurance*. From what Mr. Nixon said afterward to his companions on Air Force One, flying onward that night from Knoxville to the Western White House, it was clear that he drew needed assurance and comfort from his hour at the Reverend Billy Graham's Crusade. The President said that it was a great experience, one of the great occasions of his life. And in its way it was a great occasion, not the absurd and fraudulent event that some of us in the White House press corps thought it would be when we were told that Mr. Nixon was going to pause at Knoxville on his way to California for the Memorial Day weekend and address Youth Night at the Graham Crusade.

Beforehand and up to the moment of arrival at the stadium, there seemed to be all the makings of a fraud; of an abuse, in the worst Nixon taste, of a supposedly religious occasion. The preliminaries suggested that the President knew that it could be made to look that way and was troubled by the prospect. When his friend Billy telephoned from Knoxville on the previous Sunday and invited him, the President hesitated and said that he would have to think it over for a day or two. The Reverend Billy's clinching argument, the one that persuaded Mr. Nixon, was that the coming Youth Night offered a chance for a safe and predictably successful encounter with thousands of young people "on a campus." Some heckling would have to be expected. But it could be contained by the police, and the hecklers, who were sure to be vastly outnumbered, could be relied upon to dramatize the gulf that Mr. Nixon was so fond of talking about between them and the majority of Americans.

The political connotations that Mr. Nixon immediately attached to the visit, once he decided to risk it, enhanced the aura of contrivance. Republican Senator Howard Baker and Congressman William E. Brock, the GOP candidate for the seat of Democratic Senator Albert Gore, were asked to accompany the President, along with other Republican incumbents and candidates. The excuse that only East Tennesseans were invited fell apart when Congressman Dan Kuykendall of Memphis, which is at the farthermost border of West Tennessee, turned up with the Nixon party. Senator Gore, who was not invited, was in Knoxville the day of the visit, but he didn't show himself in Nixon's vicinity. The favored Republicans must have wondered what they got out of the trip and whether the President really wanted them along when he arrived in Knoxville. His plane landed at an isolated National Guard airstrip instead of at the nearby municipal airport, where welcomers and protesters might have assembled. His political guests were never introduced or mentioned. At the one stop along the Nixon motorcade's route from the airstrip to the stadium, the President seemed to be strained, ill at ease, apologetic, as he signed a few autographs and quickly returned to his car. He asked that the bullet proof bubbletop on the White House convertible be removed, in deference to the friendly people who lined the highway, but he did not appear to be displeased when his Secret Service escorts said that the protective top was out of order and could not be detached. It was as if he were more annoyed than pleased by the roadside throngs, the handwritten signs of welcome, the abundance of symbolic American flags; as if he knew that the promised success would come, if at all, at the stadium.

It did. It was not the President's doing: the forgettable banalities of his speech, with his tired football jokes and his unconvincing salute to "a *great* young generation" were equaled in their emptiness only by the crisp clichés in the Reverend Billy's introduction and in his sermon—his standard and (to me) inexplicably effective call to Christ and eternal life. It was the crowd, the immense and overpowering crowd, that made the occasion and made the evening for the President. It was not the predominantly young crowd that the Reverend Billy had promised, though thousands of young people were there. Most of the 70,000 faces staring down upon the President from the towering tiers of the stadium were adult and middle-aged faces, rural faces; the faces of people from the towns, the mountains and valleys of the East Tennessee country around Knoxville; the faces of people who believe in the Reverend Billy's God and live out their lives in the hope of Billy's heaven.

Most people in that part of Tennessee vote Republican, and the President drew some 20,000 more people than the Reverend Billy alone had drawn on the preceding nights. But it seemed to me that this was not, in the event, a political evening and that it had very little political meaning. What the President was said to have taken, in his talk afterward aboard Air Force One, to be an overwhelming show of approval of him and of his war, among other things, seemed to me to be more a show of massive disapproval of the young dissenters and their way of declaring their opposition to the war.

There were some 200 of them, clustered together far down the stadium from the platform, to the President's right. They were of high school and university age, though local reporters said that very few of them were from the university. They served the President exactly as the Reverend Billy had said they would. They called for "Peace Now!," they carried signs saying "Thou Shalt Not Kill," and they debased themselves and their cause with their chants of "Bullshit, Bullshit!" and (not often, but often enough to shock the Nixon party) "Fuck Richard Nixon!" The scores of city and state policemen who watched them and dogged them and arrested three of them were enforcing a 1932 state law, a relic of the Prohibition era and its bitter rows between Tennesseans who favored and opposed the legalized sale of liquor, that forbids the disruption of educational, religious, and "temperance" meetings but doesn't mention political meetings. So the hecklers, disciplined in their fashion, shouted their cries for peace and their obscenities only when the Reverend Billy introduced the President and when the President spoke. About half of them left when the President finished, and the remaining hundred or so did an interesting thing. They, boys and girls, listened as intently and with as much discernible reverence to Billy's sermon as the other youngsters and the adults in the audience did. At the end, when Billy Graham called for the nightly "commitment to Christ," perhaps 50 of the dissenters left their seats, marched silently up the football field, and took their stand beside the platform at Mr. Nixon's right. There, still silent, they raised their right arms and forefingers in the "V" for peace and thrust their signal back and forth, back and forth. In the several minutes that I stood with them, watching the President, he did not once look toward them or acknowledge their presence. While the Graham pianist played and the Graham choir softly sang, "Just as I am . . . to Thee, Oh Lamb of God, I come, I come," and hundreds young and old did come to God and Billy, the President kept his eyes fixed upon the Reverend Billy's erect and beautifully tailored back, as if it were a point of escape from the fingers of peace.

Here at his Western White House, the President was said to be still talking about and savoring the hour at the stadium. What he was said to remember, to draw from it all, was proof to him that the good people of America, his and the Reverend Billy's people, approve of him and trust him and will stay with him through the agonies of Vietnam and Indochina. One may suppose that he was thinking and believing this when he conferred with his military commanders and his Secretary of Defense and his national security adviser on the Sunday of the Memorial weekend and prepared himself to announce to the nation by television that we are winning a famous victory in Cambodia. The White House reporters, denied even a glimpse of him in California except at a brief session for photographers at the opening of the Sunday conference, indulged in long and futile hassles with Press Secretary Ronald Ziegler over what he was and was not saying for the President about the intentions and prospects in Vietnam and in all Indochina. The central intention is utterly clear: in the name of protecting the security of American forces in South Vietnam, to support in any fashion found to be necessary the steadily widening war in Indochina and the Asian forces, South Vietnamese and Cambodian and Thai, that have been dragooned into waging it for the United States. Mr. Nixon no doubt believes that his present way is the only available way, in the absence of negotiation, to the peace he surely wants. But one may wish that the President had not so totally ignored, that he had acknowledged with a single look and smile, the grubby youngsters who made the V sign for him in Knoxville.

June 13, 1970

———

Scores of arbitrary arrests, obviously designed to break up dissident student groups at the University of Tennessee, followed the President's visit and were deplored in the mildest possible fashion by a White House assistant.

XVIII

Saving Bob Finch

Bob Finch was stooped beyond his custom, and brushing his eyes with his right hand, as if he had been crying, when he walked into the White House press room at 11:12 on the morning of Saturday, June 6. Mr. Nixon was ahead of him and Under Secretary of State Elliot L. Richardson was behind him. A White House assistant who had been with them in the President's Oval Office said later that the Secretary of Health, Education, and Welfare had not been weeping but on the contrary had appeared to be as happy as he was to say in a moment that he was at being removed from HEW and transferred to the White House staff. "I am very honored, very flattered," Finch said, but he didn't look at that instant as if he were either happy, honored, or flattered. He looked to me as if he were ready to be returned, on a stretcher, to the hospital where he had been treated three weeks earlier for "a neurological disorder," attributed by his doctors to "extreme fatigue," that had numbed his arms just before he was to have confronted hundreds of HEW employes who were disillusioned with him and with the Nixon Administration. The President also appeared to be tired, drawn of face, troubled and saddened as he began by saying, "I am announcing today the first change in our Cabinet," and went on to say that

he was nominating Richardson to succeed Finch at the head of
HEW. The news photographs that soon showed three pleased and
smiling men at the pressroom podium were travesties of the actual
occasion, proof of the adage that pictures can lie.

So ended, in a public humiliation that the President could not
have intended but could not disguise, the Secretaryship of a man
whom he termed "my oldest and closest friend and associate within
the Administration." The explanations that Mr. Nixon offered then
and that Finch and White House assistants offered later provided in
their sum and in their contradictions a revealing glimpse of the
Administration at grips with and trying to resolve a painful problem. The President's explanation was quite correct, so far as it
went: he had hoped that his friend Bob Finch could serve him
simultaneously as "a personal adviser and counselor" and as the
Secretary in charge of a "huge and extremely important Department." Finding after 17 months that "this cannot be done," he had
asked Finch, and Finch had consented, "to come to the White
House on a full-time basis as Counselor to the President." Others
at the White House said that Finch had assented without serious
demur, once the President's wishes were clear to him. Finch con-
tradicted them and, characteristically, himself. He told Haynes
Johnson of the *Washington Post* that he "argued strongly" against
the change and finally agreed to it, at a meeting on the Friday
morning before the announcement, only when the President "came
on hard . . . and put me to the wall" and made it "very clear to
me [that] it was something he wanted, and wanted now." It was
"categorically untrue," Finch said in the same interview, that he
had been ousted or removed from HEW. He had instructed his
press spokesman, Baxter Omohundro, to say after the Friday session with the President that it "was absolutely untrue" that he was
about to resign.

Counselor Finch will have to do better than that. It is not that
the judicious practice of deception gets the President's men in trouble with the President, but that Secretary Finch's particular way of
practicing it at HEW tended to make him look good at the President's expense. The key to success on the Nixon staff is a faculty
for learning or sensing what Mr. Nixon wants and then working to
get it for him when he wants it in the shape he wants it. His chief
domestic assistants, John Ehrlichman and H. R. (Bob) Haldeman,
possess this faculty to the ultimate degree and it constitutes their

principal though by no means their only value to him. His two
Counselors, Bryce N. Harlow and Daniel P. Moynihan, whom
Finch now joins, are very good at it, too, and Finch will have to
master the same art and practice it in a way he never did at HEW if
he is to have the useful and happy future at the White House that
the President predicted for him and that he predicted for himself.

It is odd that this should have to be said of a man with Finch's
long background of friendship and association with the President.
They have known each other since 1947. Finch was Vice President
Nixon's administrative assistant in the Eisenhower years, and he
was still a Nixon man when he ran for lieutenant governor of California in 1966 and got more votes for that office than the head of
the ticket, Ronald Reagan, got for governor. He was a close and
frequent consultant to Nixon during the 1968 Presidential campaign, he could have had the Republican nomination for Vice President if he had wanted it, and it was by his choice that he took the
Cabinet spot at HEW instead of joining the early Nixon staff. Yet
he behaved throughout his time in the Secretaryship as if he
thought the way to please Richard Nixon was to make him look the
fool, or worse. Finch held out for the nomination of Dr. John H.
Knowles of Boston to be Assistant Secretary for health services for
weeks after it was apparent that Nixon wouldn't take him, and
finally gave way in circumstances that did neither the Secretary nor
the President credit but put the main onus on the President. The
same pattern marked the handling of other HEW appointments,
creating an impression (accurate in some cases, but not conducive
to warm HEW-White House relationships) that the President and
his staff were more responsible than Finch was for the chaos in
Finch's department. It was Finch who started the destructive talk
early last year about revising the guidelines governing school desegregation and embraced the fallacy that the way to bring Southern segregationists into line is to be nice to them. At the same time
he privately fostered the notion, not entirely false but again not calculated to improve his standing at the White House, that he was the
liberal friend of integration, fighting the good fight for it against the
President and his conservative mentor, John N. Mitchell.

Why, then, was the President moved to say of Finch, "I
regret losing him at HEW, but I need him here"? And that, as he
said to Finch and to the press, he needed him now, "in a special
capacity that has not been filled adequately for my purposes be-

fore"? The favored answers were two—that Finch's managerial and other troubles at HEW had brought him close to physical collapse, which they had; and that HEW required a Secretary with the talent for administration that Elliot Richardson is supposed to have demonstrated at State. The second consideration was a factor, but I am told at the White House that it was not decisive. HEW has been recognized for what it is, an inherently unmanageable conglomerate of vaguely related social agencies, since it was put together in 1953, and serious thought is being given to breaking it up into more rational segments. I am also told at the White House that what I take to be the primary reason for Finch's transfer and demotion is no more than a secondary reason.

My theory is that Robert Finch's enforced move to the White House is connected with the rapid and extraordinary process of awakening that has occurred there. The President, his chief assistants and even Vice President Agnew have been made aware to an extent they haven't been before that disaffection with Vietnam policy and with many aspects of domestic Nixon policy is deep and genuine and serious; that it is not to be dismissed any longer, in the Agnew fashion, as merely the creation of hostile media and of "criminal misfits." One of the few Nixon men at the Administration's top level who have realized this all along, and said so, is Labor Secretary George Shultz, who is coming into the White House orbit at the head of the expanded Bureau of the Budget (to be monstrously called, after July 1, the Office of Management and Budget).

Finch is another. Despite the flaws in his performance at HEW, he projects the look and feel of a humane and sensitive politician; not the committed "liberal" that the national press has often taken him to be and that he himself has sometimes pretended to be, but still a Nixon man who may be counted upon to communicate with and impress young, black, and simply principled Americans who are repelled by the likes of Spiro Agnew and Attorney General Mitchell. When the President said that he expected to take Counselor Finch with him on his travels, "for general preparation of speeches and other statements," he did not (I am told) intend to cast his new adviser in the menial role that the remark seemed to imply. Finch is expected to "generate ideas" for major Nixon speeches, review staff-written drafts, and generally assist the President in an effort to be, or least appear to be, more responsive to the dissents and doubts of troubled America than he has been.

This is a time of sudden change at the top, and it's no time for hard judgment of the changes. The case of Commissioner of Education James E. Allen, Jr., who was fired by Finch at the President's order, is in point. He had shown himself to be a devout integrationist, a genuine "liberal," but, in the hostile Nixon atmosphere, a weak advocate. He should have quit months earlier.

June 20, 1970

XIX

Updating Welfare

The chubby face of Russell Long of Louisiana, chairman of the Senate Finance Committee, was aglow with righteous intent and goodwill when he said on May 1, at the close of the first phase of hearings on the Nixon welfare reforms: "We do want to pass this bill. We would like to pass a bill which takes into consideration everything that private employers can be expected to do, everything that state governments can be expected to do, everything that other federal agencies can be expected to do, as a result of this overall effort." Senator John J. Williams of Delaware, a renowned Republican champion of thrift and efficiency who retires this year, said that existing federal and state welfare aids to the poor "must all be considered and taken together" in any reform bill that he would support. Health, Education, and Welfare Secretary Robert H. Finch, who had no idea then that he would be replaced within six weeks, protested that "we cannot solve all of these problems" with the bill before the committee. But he promised that after further study "we will come forward with a broader something . . . and work with you to have an omnibus bill to work out this problem."

The "broader something" that emerged in mid-June from weeks of frantic effort at the White House, HEW, the Budget Bureau, and the Departments of Labor and Agriculture is not the "omnibus bill" that the Senate committee compelled Finch to promise. It is, instead, a mix of hasty amendments to the Nixon welfare bill as it was passed by the House and of a promise to come up by February 15, 1971, with additional legislation. But it must be granted that the Administration's new proposals constitute the "historic" advance in welfare policy that White House Counselor Daniel P. Moynihan said they do. They should but may not save the original Nixon program of guaranteed minimal income for welfare and "working poor" families from the sudden death that both Republicans and Democrats on the Finance Committee seemed to be preparing for it in May.

Whether the family assistance plan survives, and whether the proposed addition to it of the nation's first federally subsidized system of health insurance for the poor has a chance of enactment in 1971, depends mainly upon Senators Long, Williams, and Herman Talmadge of Georgia. They are the committeemen who principally forced the Administration to take back its family income bill and reconcile it with related food-stamp housing, and medical programs. If these senators don't buy the offered mixture, and they were slow to say whether they would or not, the revised family income bill will either die in the committee or come out of it so changed that the House will be unlikely to accept the altered version. Chances of reviving the Nixon income guarantee in the new Congress that convenes in 1971 will be dim, and the prospects of combining it with subsidized insurance will be even dimmer if both programs have to be sold in one enormous package. That is why it was said at the White House that "we are dead serious about wanting a bill this year" and that, if only the Finance Committee will allow the Senate to act upon a reasonable facsimile of the Nixon welfare bill, the Administration will be "prepared to go as far as anybody wants to go in the Congresses to come" with further welfare refinements.

The miracle of the 1970 congressional session is that the House Ways and Means Committee and then the full House approved the Nixon income measure with few substantive changes, none of them destructive and many of them improvements. The man who wrought the miracle is Wilbur Mills of Arkansas, chairman of Ways and Means, and he is quietly abetting the Administration in its warnings to the Senate Finance Committee that it had better leave what he has come to think of as *his* bill largely intact if any welfare reform is to be enacted this year. The House bill preserves the basic guarantee that every family of one or two parents and one or more dependent children will have some cash income, paid in federal dollars, from a minimum of $1000 for one parent and one dependent child to $1600 for the "family of four" (two parents, two children) that is cited as the typical example. Earned income up to $720 a year and half of any further earned income up to a "poverty level" varying with the size of the family may be retained by "the working poor" without deduction from the basic $500 for each adult and $300 for each dependent child that the federal government guarantees. The House eliminated a requirement that niggardly states, meaning those in the Deep South, continue to put up at least half of what they had been paying in state welfare costs, and several of them are now relieved of the painful necessity of contributing a penny to their welfare families, most of them black. But this concession is offset by substantial increases in what they would have to pay to assist dependent aged, blind, and disabled adults, and on balance the Southern states get less relative benefit from increased federal welfare contributions than do the states— California, Illinois, and New York, for example—that have the most generous assistance programs and the heaviest costs. The requirement that employable family heads, excepting mothers with children under six years of age, must register for and accept any "suitable" jobs or training for jobs, remains in the bill and has been tightened since the Administration proposed it. This feature continues to disturb some liberal defenders of the bill, but the protections against arbitrary abuse of the power to determine what is "suitable" have been strengthened, at least in theory, and the word itself though not the intent was dropped from the House bill.

The Senate committee complaints that resulted in the innovative insurance proposal were originally aimed at removing anomalies which, as the critics showed from the Administration's data, make total dependence upon welfare more profitable in an embarrassing number of cases than working for a part of a poor family's income would be. In too many instances, the Administration's witnesses had to admit, very small increases in earned income could and did render welfare beneficiaries ineligible for assistance ranging from food-stamps to rental subsidies and federal-state Medicaid. In response, the Administration proposes to meld the food-stamp program with family assistance, transfer it from Agriculture to HEW, and provide that the small portion of food-stamp costs charged to beneficiaries may be deducted from their basic welfare payments. Instead of chopping off rent subsidies and the right to live in public housing at an arbitrary level of earned income, the proportion of the subsidized rent paid by the renting families would rise with increasing incomes. For the wholly dependent families now eligible for free medical care in states that have adopted Medicaid, a wholly new program of subsidized insurance would be substituted and "working poor" families who now get no public help at all would be eligible for it, too. Between five and six million families including 25 to 30 million individuals would be covered, at an estimated federal cost beginning at $1.9 billion a year in fiscal 1972 and rising to $2.8 billion by 1975. Many details still have to be worked out and submitted in the legislation promised by early 1971. But the outline is clear in the proposal as it emerged in June.

It offers benefitted families up to $500 worth of more or less comprehensive insurance, including hospital and some out-patient care, on the scale that a private buyer of medical insurance gets for $500 a year. For families with no income or (for the "typical" family of four) no more than $1600 a year, the insurance would be free and paid entirely by the federal government. For families with higher incomes (between $1600 and $3920 for the same family of four), participation would be compulsory and up to $160 of the $500 annual premium would be deducted from their federal income supplements. For those with incomes above $3920 and up to a cut-off point of $5620 a year, participation would be voluntary and those at the top of the scale would have to pay the full $500 if they chose the coverage. If the compulsory deduction from assistance payments to the middle-poor bothers Congress, the Administration is prepared to recommend a compensatory increase of $100 in the basic level of federal income supplements. How the enormous increase in the demand for medical services that would result is to be met is a problem the Administration leaves to future solution. That and many other questions are sure to be raised. But they are outweighed by the real significance of the proposal, which is that it could put the country on the way to the comprehensive national health care that should have been instituted long ago.

June 27, 1970

———

Mr. Nixon promised in early 1971 to submit to Congress a greatly broadened national health program, incorporating medical insurance for the poor with proposals aimed at increasing both the quality and the amount of medical care for everyone.

Rearranging
Furniture

Secretary of Labor George P. Shultz was conducting a meeting of
the Cabinet Committee on School Desegregation in the Executive
Office Building, next door to the White House, when he was told on
the afternoon of June 4 that two of the President's assistants, John
D. Ehrlichman and H. R. Haldeman, wanted to see him. The circumstances and the message were not unusual. Shultz was the vice
chairman of the committee and he lately had spent so much time
on it and on other Presidential assignments, many of which came to
him through Ehrlichman or Haldeman, that his subordinates at the
Labor Department had begun to say with some irritation that he
might as well move to the White House and become by title what
he was close to being in fact, a staff assistant to the President.

When Shultz joined Ehrlichman and Haldeman in Haldeman's
office in the West Wing of the White House, just down the hall
from Mr. Nixon's Oval Office, they gave him a piece of news that
any other President might have been expected to impart in person

to his Secretary of Labor. They told him that the President had decided to make him the director of the new Office of Management and Budget, which was to replace the old Bureau of the Budget on July 1. He was to be considered a member of the President's senior staff, he was to have the prestige of a West Wing office, and no less a personage than Caspar Weinberger, the chairman of the Federal Trade Commission, was to be the deputy director of OMB. Weinberger, who after only five months at FTC was well along with a thorough reorganization of it, would relieve Shultz of much of the administrative burden at OMB and free him for the larger task of monitoring and improving management wherever improvement seemed to be needed throughout the federal bureaucracy. Shultz later gave his astonished associates at the Labor Department the impression that Ehrlichman and Haldeman didn't ask him to take the job; in effect, they told him on behalf of the President to take it. He said that the news hit him like "a bombshell" and he added, "I was in no position to refuse," a remark that indicated to his friends at Labor that he obeyed the President's command with something less than total glee. His wife told an interviewer that she was shocked and that, with the family buying a new house just then, she was unhappy about the cut in salary from a Cabinet Secretary's $60,000 to the OMB director's $42,500 a year.

It was the beginning, secret at the time, of topside shifts that within a week gave the Nixon White House at least the appearance of a new facade. The next day the President ordered his friend and associate of many years, Health, Education, and Welfare Secretary Robert H. Finch, to relinquish that post and tapped Under Secretary of State Elliot Richardson to replace him at HEW. Finch moved to the White House, into a West Wing office next to Ehrlichman's and around a corner from the one prepared for Shultz. Both Finch, now a Counselor to the President, and Shultz were appointed to the new Domestic Council, a Cabinet-level body authorized in the same reorganization act that established the OMB. (One sees why they didn't call it the Bureau of Management and Budget—BOMB.) The Domestic Council is intended to do in the preparation of domestic policy alternatives and recommendations for the President more or less what the National Security Council does or is supposed to do in matters of foreign policy. John Ehrlichman, already the President's assistant for domestic affairs, is the Domestic Council's executive director and, in its policy area, the counterpart of Henry Kissinger. The changes, institutional and personal, bring to a climax but predictably do not terminate Mr. Nixon's tireless endeavor to prove that the federal government can be managed efficiently—and to prove also that, as he maintains with uncharacteristic passion, efficient management is the key to making it the "more responsive and the more effective government" that he says "the people deserve."

The institutional changes, important though they were, interested and preoccupied Mr. Nixon's White House people much less than the personal changes did. For this there were reasons that went beyond a predilection for gossip.

It is accepted at the White House that the transfer of Robert Finch was primarily a rescue operation. It was timed to save him from the difficulties of administering a huge department that had brought him to the verge of collapse and, by the same shift, to place HEW in the charge of a Secretary who was thought to be a strong administrator. Shultz, an academic specialist in economics and industrial relations and management before he was brought to Washington from the University of Chicago, was transferred from Labor to the White House primarily because he had impressed the President with a diversity of talents for management and for the analysis of policy and administrative problems. He is expected, as the President said and as the reorganization act envisages, to superimpose upon the replaced bureau's budgetary responsibilities an overriding responsibility for improving federal management at every level, whether by internal reform of departments and agencies or by reorganization and consolidation of some of them.

But there was more to the reassignments of Finch and Shultz than these reasons indicate. Mr. Nixon was in need of men like them at the White House, both for public effect and the effect upon restive and doubting people on his own staff and elsewhere in government. I have written of the awakening at the White House to the realities, the breadth, and the gravity of dissent in America. There has been an awakening as well to the fact that the hard face turned to America from the White House by the Administration's Agnews, its John Mitchells, its hardly known but somehow sensed young pragmatists from advertising, the law, Wall Street and journalism aggravated the dissent and the problems it was making for Mr. Nixon, who had proved to be a considerable aggravator in his own right. The same face, the harsh conservatism that it projected, was also making trouble for the President within his own establishment. Cambodia compounded the trouble. Three of Henry Kissinger's young men quit, partly because of the Cambodia decision, and the departure of two senior Kissinger assistants for other reasons was made less painful for them by that decision. Arthur Klabenoff, a talented young assistant to Counselor Daniel P. Moynihan, left in quiet protest. A substantial number of other White House assistants, mostly young and including some of the brightest people in the place, were audibly wondering whether and how long they could abide what seemed to them to be repellent turns in both domestic and foreign policy and the emphasis placed upon those turns by the Agnew rhetoric. The doubts and discontents were shared by men who on occasion work directly for the President and he must have been aware that he might be embarrassed by a small but noticeable wave of resignations.

Something had to be done and Mr. Nixon did it with the appointment of Shultz and Finch to the White House staff. Both of them are men of moderate cast, liberals by the Nixon standard. The effect, however incidental it may have been to the President's primary purposes, was instantaneous and unmistakable. The men of whom I write—it would be a useless disservice to them and to the country to name them—took immediate heart. They read into both appointments (rather wishfully, I suspect) a signal that the President meant well according to their lights, after all, and even that he himself and his basic policies might be changing for what they consider to be better. Even the Vice President, they thought they had reason to hope, might be toning down his more divisive rhetoric and becoming, if not bearable, at least not altogether unbearable.

There were other aspects, less interesting but worthy of note. How, for instance, would John Ehrlichman and George Shultz get along in what had previously seemed to be a single role of domestic dominance for Ehrlichman but must now become a dual role? The guess encouraged at the White House, and probably a sound one, is that they will get along well enough. John Ehrlichman, who was an obscure Seattle attorney specializing in zoning and land-use law until Mr. Nixon installed him at the White House, has the faculty of attracting power to himself without overtly grabbing for it and he strikes the assistants who work with him as the sort of man who won't fight against a reasonable sharing of it with Director Shultz. By the terms of the reorganization act, and by the President's plainly stated wish, Ehrlichman heads the "institutional staff" through which all formal domestic policy recommendations, presumably including those from Shultz, must pass on the way to the Oval Office. Most people at the White House expected Ehrlichman to enlarge his already substantial staff, once the Domestic Council came into being, and that in fact was his intention until Shultz was assigned to OMB and the White House. Now Ehrlichman is planning to cut back his present staff, trimming it down to the assistants whom he considers to be particularly adept at policy formulation, and transferring to Shultz (if he will take them) the ones who are identified in the main as "operators." With this canny approach, Ehrlichman simultaneously strengthens his claim to the formal policy role and allays the suspicions of domestic Cabinet Secretaries who may have feared that he would stand more firmly than he does now between them and the President. Shultz in his new capacity could be the assistant they really have to worry about, but his equable and easy temperament is such that they probably will give him the benefit of the doubt until further notice.

An episode well known to them all indicates that the further notice is bound to come if Shultz does the job of managerial monitoring that the President expects him to do. At the President's request, Shultz played an active part in the handling of the postal strikes in New York City and elsewhere. Postmaster General Winton (Red) Blount tolerated Shultz's participation so long as the crisis was acute and the President was in overall charge of handling it. Once the strikes began to subside and the President withdrew, Blount made it known that Shultz should go back to Labor and leave the Post Office Department to the Postmaster General. Shultz did, although the wage negotiations that then ensued could have been said to be in his bailiwick. Others at the White House, Ehrlichman included, anticipate that similar frictions are certain to develop as Shultz gets into the swing of managerial oversight. People with a taste for such conflicts are awaiting the day when Director Shultz tells George Romney, the crusty Secretary of Housing and Urban Development, that his department could use some administrative reform along Shultz lines.

There also is bound to be pain among the professional budget-

NIXON WATCH II

eers of the replaced and expanded Budget Bureau. But their discomfort is nothing to the pain that Mr. Nixon will suffer if the possibility that he showed himself to be aware of when he announced Shultz's appointment is realized. The President remarked that the creation of OMB "will have been a great mistake" if it turns out to be "just another layer on the top of too much government already."

July 4, 1970

XXI

Why Cambodia?

San Clemente, California

The country should be grateful to Mr. Nixon for the orgy of explanation and justification with which he celebrated the withdrawal of American ground troops from Cambodia. It was one hell of a show, informative in ways that the President could not have intended. His chief propagandist, Communications Director Herbert Klein, assembled 38 news editors and executives at the Western White House for a massive indoctrinal session and broke the rule of secrecy that usually governs such briefings by identifying the principal indoctrinator as the President's assistant for national security affairs, Henry Kissinger. Then came a written summary report in the President's name, another briefing for the working press, and a nationally televised "conversation" with three network commentators. The total performance, overdone and transparently contrived as it was, indicated a state of profound official unease and defensiveness about the Cambodian operation.

The restless, jumpy quality that marked Mr. Nixon's behavior when he announced his decision to undertake the operation was again in evidence. His staff first said that he would be too busy with his preparations for his network "conversation" to greet Mrs. Nixon when she returned from a mercy mission to Peru and landed at a nearby Marine Corps airbase. He changed his mind, made the short chopper trip to greet her, choppered back to the Western White House, and immediately departed for Los Angeles, there to hole up in a hotel for 24 hours instead of completing the preparations at his secluded office and home on the San Clemente coast.

All of it was useful, just the same. In conjunction with earlier statements and background supplements, the performance provided an authoritative insight into Nixon policy and purposes, not only in Southeast Asia but in the larger world. What follows is a series of conclusions derived from the proffered official explanations, public and private, of why the President ordered the Cambodian "incursion" and of what he hoped to accomplish with it.

It was intended in part to demonstrate to three adversaries—the Communist governments in Hanoi, Peking, and Moscow—that they cannot and must not assume that the course of American policy under Richard Nixon is always and safely predictable. Most of the time and on most levels of policy, we have been told at the White House, the President intends and wants to be steady and predictable. But if ever the adversaries of the United States, and most especially Hanoi, get the idea that nothing that they may do to offend or provoke the United States will affect what the President does, then the planning of the adversaries becomes altogether too easy for them and the pressure upon the United States becomes ever greater. A minimum of unpredictability is desirable, but that minimum is essential. Mr. Nixon, so reasoning, knew when he ordered the Cambodian operation that his action would have an effect upon the Soviet government. It would be well for the United States if the Soviet and other adversaries were made to realize, perhaps to an extent that they had not recently realized, that it could be dangerous for all concerned to let problems and situations much wider than those in Indochina remain static and unresolved, on an assumption that the United States would do nothing about them if the other parties didn't. Thus, precisely because it was unexpected, the action in Cambodia could indirectly improve the possibilities of progress toward big-power sponsorship of a negotiated Arab-Israeli settlement and, for another example with global significance, in the effort at the SALT talks to limit nuclear armaments by agreement. The officials who said this on the President's behalf also said, with emphasis and with no discernible sense of contradiction, that achieving the indicated effect was not a specific objective of the Cambodian operation and was not a factor in the President's decision to order it. There was no intention, they said, to confront the Soviet Union with anything or to trigger it into concessions on other issues.

The President made the completion of the American withdrawal the occasion for a renewed and intensified call for a negotiated peace. It was said when the attack upon the Cambodian sanctuaries was ordered that it just might persuade Hanoi that negotiation was preferable to continued warfare. The hope underlying the President's newest statements is a little, but only a little, stronger than it was 60 days ago. It rests mainly, in the anguished words of a Nixon staff adviser, upon a conviction that the North Vietnamese simply cannot be the only people in history who have no regard whatever for material losses and difficulties, and it is tempered, now as in the past, by a realization that North Vietnam's rulers and fighters have displayed a courage, a stubbornness, that may indicate that for them negotiation in our meaning of the term is impossible. Mr. Nixon's advisers deduce from the slim available evidence that Hanoi is reassessing its situation. They also deduce—they say they have not been told—that the Soviet government prefers negotiation now or soon to indefinite continuance of the war, and that it may be suggesting as much to the Hanoi government. The recall to Hanoi of a few of its key ambassadors has been noted, with hope but no certain knowledge that this indicates that Hanoi is as worried as our logic tells the President and his advisers it ought to be.

A factor in the slight revival of hope, short of declared expectation, is a shift of nuance in the published Nixon terms that the President included in his April 20 speech, announcing his plan to withdraw 150,000 more Americans from South Vietnam by May 1, 1971. Always before April 20, he had stipulated that free elections in South Vietnam must figure in any negotiated settlement. In April he said, without mentioning elections, that a negotiated "political solution" should be possible and could be acceptable. It was the farthest he had been willing to go toward a public indication that the undeclared equivalent of a coalition postwar government might be negotiated if the North Vietnamese were prepared to bargain in Paris. To the dismay of Henry Kissinger and others at the White House, the press was slow to recognize and publicize a major piece of bait. Their disappointment suggested that the President was relying upon the press, rather than upon the private channels that have been used in the past to convey secret intimations of American "flexibility," to impress upon Hanoi the implied significance of the change. The reason why the nuance was not spelled out directly to Hanoi illuminates the Administration's dilemma and indicates that it in part had made the dilemma for itself. The Nixon-Kissinger theory has been that any explicit or direct show of concession, beyond what the Administration thinks it has already conceded, in advance of substantive negotiation would inspire Hanoi to hold out for more and more concessions, to the point of American surrender without negotiation.

Thousands of words were addressed here publicly and privately to the question of what the President intends for and in Cambodia. He intends what he has intended since he took the war from South Vietnam into Cambodia. He intends to restrict himself and the United States only to his promise that no more American ground troops will be used there, and otherwise to do with air and Asian action whatever he deems necessary to deny effective possession and control of Cambodia to the Communists. He hopes to accomplish this objective without committing the United States to the preservation of a non-Communist Cambodian government. But this and all other restrictions upon the American presence in Cambodia are subject to change if the North Vietnamese and the Vietcong raise the level of their military action and threat to a point that the President thinks intolerable.

The effect upon me of the elaborate apology for the Nixon decision was to affirm my initial conclusion that it was madness. The Administration's stated rationale for the attack upon the North Vietnamese border sanctuaries is that the Communists had turned inward upon Cambodia from those sanctuaries and were threatening to make the whole country a base for heightened attack upon the Americans in South Vietnam. If this is so—and the case for its being so seems to me extremely weak—it follows that the United States is committed to indefinite battle in Cambodia to preserve it from Communist control. The President's own briefers made nonsense of his repeated assertions that he had not intended to widen the war and in fact had not widened it. They said, in boasting of recently reduced American casualties in South Vietnam, that the war had moved westward, into Cambodia, and implied a hope that it will continue to be focused there. In terms of national responsibility, whether the President succeeds in confining American military action to air support—his pledge that it will be limited to air "interdiction" of enemy supply lines is a transparent euphemism—and in holding the ground with Cambodian, South Vietnamese, and possibly Thai forces, is irrelevant. Mr. Nixon's claim that he has achieved in Cambodia the greatest military success of the Vietnam war is tenable only if it be granted that the way to diminish the American involvement and to end the war is to expand it.

July 11, 1970

XXII

Agnew
and Red Meat

In and about the White House at mid-year, the inquirer finds cautious agreement with the proposition that Vice President Spiro T. Agnew has been persuaded to moderate his line of talk and generally to change his public performance for the better. This is a very sensitive subject, one that is discussed with the greatest care by the President's and the Vice President's assistants. They say that the President has not told his Vice President to change in any way and that neither of the only two Nixon assistants, John D. Ehrlichman and H. R. Haldeman, who might speak for the President to the Vice President in such a matter, has told him to, either. It is still said, as it has been ever since the Administration took office, that Mr. Nixon and Mr. Agnew seldom have or make occasion for private discussion of this or any other subject. They rarely meet, except at formal Cabinet and similar gatherings, and such talk as they have with each other is mostly by telephone. So far as anyone at the White House or in the Agnew premises across the way in the

Executive Office Building admits or seems to know, Mr. Nixon has not restated to the Vice President in person the rule that the President publicly recommended to "all of the members of this Administration" at his press conference on May 8: "When the action is hot, keep the rhetoric cool."

There has been some change in the Agnew performance since then, but not nearly as much as I thought there had been when I began asking about it at the White House. All that it amounts to is the recent omission from Mr. Agnew's formal speeches of references to "impudent snobs," "rotten apples," "criminal activists," "hardcore dissidents" and the like in terms that invite students, restive blacks, antiwar protesters, and the myriad others who question this or that Nixon attitude and policy to assume that the Vice President is indicting all of them. It reflects no change at all in Mr. Agnew himself and in his conception of what a Vice President of the United States may responsibly and usefully say. He has taken a little more care with the way he says it, but in his less formal utterances he gives evidence that both the omissions and the newly discreet elisions of the same old points may be transitory. Yet the change, small and illusory though it has been, is considered at the White House to be significant, and a study of the factors that have brought it about reveals a good deal about the Vice President and about the Nixon-Agnew relationship.

The pressures upon Agnew that have led to this show of moderation predate the Nixon establishment's concern with the appearance it was giving of crass indifference to the dissents and divisions that trouble the country. A quite different kind of concern developed in the vicinity of Mr. Nixon's Oval Office in early 1970. The concern was neither with what Agnew was saying nor with its corrosive and divisive effects upon the public and the country as such. It was with the impression, then close to becoming a fact, that Spiro T. Agnew rather than Richard Nixon was beginning to personify the Nixon Administration and to preempt, in the public mind, the President's right and duty to declare and expound the Nixon position on major issues. The Nixon assistants who felt this concern had or at least disclosed to their associates no thought that Agnew might actually be positioning himself to compete with the President for the 1972 nomination. They did note, without pleasure, the growing assumption among Republican politicians in the South and elsewhere that Spiro Agnew had suddenly become so popular with his and Mr. Nixon's Middle America that the President had no choice but to keep him on the 1972 ticket. But the conscious and expressed concern had to do only with the Administration identity.

An episode in the weeks preceding Mr. Nixon's March 24 statement of his school desegregation policy illustrates the nature and gravity of the concern. That statement was first conceived and drafted as a speech to be delivered by the Vice President in Atlanta. The central issues that it involved, basically whether to commit the Administration to a final drive for adequate integration in the South or—as was proposed in one of the drafts—to question whether the pains of integration were worth the social and political cost, were hotly argued within the Nixon staff. But they were overshadowed in the preliminary stage by the question, also seriously debated, of whether Agnew or Nixon should deliver so important a policy statement. The decision was that Nixon should deliver it, the Agnew speech was scrapped, and one of the reasons was that the originally intended course would have further enhanced the Vice President's disturbingly formidable stature.

Recent happenings suggest a mutual desire to promote an appearance of both personal and philosophical separateness. Mr. Nixon must have known that the Agnew rhetoric would come to mind when he spoke of "the generation gap" to 14,000 Jaycees and their wives in St. Louis and said to them: "I charge you, I urge you, to do everything you can, not to make the gap bigger, not to set up a hostile confrontation, but to give to young people the understanding of our system that they need." When the Nixon party arrived in California from St. Louis for a stay at the Western White House, a pool reporter representing the entire press misunderstood the President to say in the Agnew manner that Washington journalists "talk to each other" and fall into a "sort of intellectual incest." After a tape recording established that Mr. Nixon had actually said that "we" in Washington, himself included, suffer from "intellectual incest" and ought to get around the country, his press assistants frantically corrected the mistaken report and said they wanted to make certain that "an Agnew type of remark" was not attributed to the President. Soon after Agnew called upon a young and rather crudely outspoken black appointee to the Nixon commission on campus disorders to resign, the President's new Counselor, Robert Finch, and the commission chairman, former Governor William

Scranton of Pennsylvania, marched straight from a talk with Mr. Nixon to the White House press room in Washington and assured reporters that the President was satisfied with the appointment.

The Vice President's former chief assistant, C. Stanley Blair, who resigned in order to run for election to Agnew's old job as Governor of Maryland, regularly attended the senior staff meetings that begin each working day at the White House. Blair's successor, Arthur Sommer, attends only by invitation and is seldom invited. The Agnew press spokesman, Herbert Thompson, was originally on the staff of the President's Director of Communications, Herbert Klein. Thompson has been removed from the Klein staff and now reports only to Agnew. The Vice President diminished his dependence upon the Nixon staff of speech writers by hiring a writer of his own and shifting Thompson from press relations to speech drafting. Some of Thompson's press duties are being assumed by Roy Goodearle, a former advance man who was transferred from the Nixon staff to the Agnew staff during the 1968 campaign. Whether Goodearle is Agnew's man or Nixon's man on the Agnew staff may be a moot point with White House reporters. In Jules Witcover's account of the 1968 campaign, *The Resurrection of Richard Nixon,* Goodearle is quoted as saying at a staff celebration after the Nixon victory, "Why don't we all get a member of the press and beat them up? I'm tired of being nice to them."

Agnew's share in the White House awakening and widened contact that followed the antiwar rally in Washington on May 9 and the student killings at Kent State University affected him as it affected everyone around Nixon. At a session in his office with Walter Heller and 10 other senior professors from the University of Minnesota, he listened with attentive respect to their protestations that his invective, the total image that he had been casting, had materially contributed to the deep, growing, and dangerous alienation of students and academics who by no stretch of reason could be numbered with the President's "campus bums" and Agnew's "criminal activists." He pleaded that he had been misrepresented and misunderstood, that he had never intended to be divisive in the way they said he had been, and he acknowledged that he perhaps had a duty to speak so that he would not be misunderstood. His staff later sent each of the professors the texts of 15 of his speeches, including four or five of the famously abrasive gems. Agnew was immensely pleased by a return letter from one of the Minnesota callers who conceded that the whole of what he had said was less offensive than the reported excerpts had been. The subsequent care with his language has not applied to the printed press and to such public figures as Senator Fulbright, former Defense Secretary Clark Clifford, and retired Ambassador Averell Harriman. Some of his attacks have been as vicious, as twisted in fact and innuendo, as ever. But the victims are fair game, in a sense that the dissenting young and black and poor are not, and if the Vice President were judged only by the speeches he delivered in June and July, he might be said to have undergone a constructive though modest change.

But Agnew denies himself that basis for judgment with his penchant for talking at length about himself, preferably on television. Then he documents characteristics that may be only deduced from his speeches. For all of his claims to respect the right of dissent, he is offended by any criticism of or attack upon established authority, particularly if it is the President's authority. He rejects the notion that a Vice President's "right" of free speech may be inhibited by his position in ways that a critical professor's or commentator's right is not inhibited. He hungers for publicity, says whatever he has to say to get it, ignores the possibility that a silent and unnoticed Vice President may at times be more useful than a vocal and publicized Vice President. Complaining that his "bland" speeches were poorly reported, he told a BBC interviewer: "So, in a desire to be heard, I have to throw them what people in American politics call a little red meat once in a while, and hope that in spite of the damaging context in which those remarks are often repeated, that other things that I think are very important will also appear." The same interviewer asked him about his notorious statement that some Americans should be separated "from our society with no more regret than we should feel over discarding rotten apples." Agnew answered: "There are people in our society who should be separated and discarded. . . . We're always going to have a certain number of people in our community who have no desire to achieve, who have no desire to even fit in in an amicable way with the rest of society; and these people should be separated from the community. Not in a callous way, but they should be separated as

far as any idea that their opinion shall have any effect on the course
we follow."

There spoke a Vice President who, thanks to Richard Nixon,
could be and, to say the very least, would not mind being the next
President of the United States.

July 25, 1970

XXIII

Southern Comfort

At the fourth informal press conference that the President had called in his Oval Office, free from the constraints of television and the thought of all those watching millions, Mr. Nixon served himself very well. He was at ease, serious, seemingly candid without once saying that he was going to be perfectly candid. His hands were under good control. He seldom looked his questioners in the eye, but his downward gaze added to the impression of considered care with every answer. He caught the reporters by surprise and didn't have to deal with many vexing questions. He appeared to harden further his hardening line on Vietnam—but in terms that, given future need, could be reconciled with a softened approach to a negotiated peace. He renewed his claim to liberalism on foreign trade (against import quotas, excepting a quota for his Southern textile friends). He stepped up his campaign against the Big Spenders in Congress (leaving to the Republican leaders in that body the actual use of the term and its application to Democrats only). And, in the most interesting performance of the day, he brought to a gentle halt the tendency among commentators and reporters to bury the Southern Strategy. He removed, for the discerning, any doubt that there has been a Southern Strategy and that there is going to continue to be one.

Mr. Nixon did not say this, of course. He said the opposite, defining the strategy in the way that he and subordinate Republicans have been defining it since he won the Presidency with it in 1968. He and his Administration, he said, are pursuing "what the South has wanted and what the South deserves, a one-nation policy—not a Southern strategy and not a Northern strategy, but a one-nation strategy."

Two elements have been and still are necessary for the successful maintenance of this line. They are the gullibility of white Southern segregationists, founded in their and all white Southerners' need for unceasing reassurance that they are not all that different from everybody else, and Mr. Nixon's skill at the practice of deceit for what he holds to be essential and constructive purposes. He double-crossed his Southern supporters in 1968, he has continued to do so since he took office, and the immediate reaction of one of them, Senator Strom Thurmond of South Carolina, to his open and unabashed resumption of the exercise suggests that the President can count upon it working as well for him this year and in 1972 as it did two years ago.

Senator Thurmond, having just savaged the President for deceiving the South in the matter of school desegregation, took it all back after the press conference and thanked Mr. Nixon for doing the white South a favor that he had only pretended to do. "I am pleased," the Senator said, surely knowing better but finding it politic to pretend he didn't, "that the President has reversed the Justice Department on its plans to send carpet-bagging lawyers and marshals into the South in anticipation of trouble over school desegregation." Thurmond had some but not much more reason to note with pleasure "that the Internal Revenue Service is rapidly approving tax-exempt status for private schools that declare an open admissions policy." The Senator was on wholly sound ground only when he said in conclusion: "The prompt manner in which the President has moved in these sensitive areas will be appreciated by his friends in the South." The record in and since 1968 entitles Mr. Nixon to expect that his manner will indeed be appreciated by enough Southerners for his political purposes, even when the reality awakens his deluded constituents once again to the fact that there's less to appreciate than he keeps promising.

The comedy enacted by the President and the Senator, and the preceding record on school desegregation, present liberal and integrationist critics of the Administration with a peculiar problem. If they are to understand what goes on and also are to be fair in judgment, they must grant the Administration credit for surprisingly strong action toward desegregation after a period of damaging inaction, without being so guileless as to grant that the action has been taken in good faith. It has been taken in the worst of faith. It has been and will continue to be limited to what statutory law, court rulings, and a third factor—Mr. Nixon's personal and political need for credibility in the nation as a whole—require the Administration to do. As I indicated previously, consideration was given at the White House in early 1970 to justifying a policy of curtailed integration in the South with a plea that anything more wouldn't be worth the pain. That course was rejected by the President, a stronger though not the strongest possible policy was adopted, and the action taken since then has been no less substantial and no less beneficial because it is required.

Mr. Nixon allowed white Southerners to believe in 1968, and Senator Thurmond told them that they could safely believe, that a Nixon Administration would let them get by with "freedom-of-choice" plans of token integration that the courts and federal enforcement agencies had held to be patent frauds. With its wobbly handling of the problem in 1969, the Administration conveyed an impression that this was indeed its purpose. A Cabinet desegregation committee set up in February and headed by Vice President Agnew was expected in the South (and by me, among others) to cater more to white prejudice than to the law's requirement. A Nixon policy statement on March 24 seemed to promise the least possible enforcement of integration. So the shock in the holdout sections of the Deep South was profound when Jerris Leonard, the Assistant Attorney General for civil rights, and other Nixon spokesmen put white segregationists on notice that their only remaining choice was voluntary, cooperative compliance with statutory and judicial commands to integrate their segregated schools, or compliance to be enforced by court orders and the termination of federal funds. The required integration would be far from complete. But it would be enough to accomplish, as the Administration said, the effective end of dual and formally segregated public school systems in the South at the opening of the 1970–71 school term. A spate of suits against the states of Georgia and Mississippi, and against individual school districts in Mississippi, Tennessee, and Texas, demonstrated that the Administration meant business. In Southern minds, these actions and the threat of more to come reduced to nothing the little comfort that could be taken from the accompanying assurances that integration was going to be enforced nationally, wherever the deliberate segregation of public schools could be proved.

The climactic shock came on July 10 when, at the President's instruction and after prolonged debate within the Administration, the Internal Revenue Service announced that private schools established throughout the Deep South to escape integration could no longer count upon exemption from federal taxes as a matter of right. As recently as May 8, the Justice Department had taken the opposite position in a brief asking a federal court to dismiss an injunction forbidding the grant of tax exemption to segregated private schools in Mississippi. Now, the President himself proclaimed through IRS, schools eligible for exemption from taxes on their own incomes and for tax-exempt contributions by donors would have to adopt and publicly declare a policy of open admission to whites and blacks alike. Attorney General Mitchell and his assistant, Leonard, disclosed in newspaper interviews that upwards of 100 Justice Department attorneys, federal marshals, and other civil-rights enforcers were to be sent into the South to monitor the integration of previously segregated schools in the fall. Senator Thurmond raged, on the Senate floor and in a personal encounter with Mitchell. Thurmond and Clarke Reed, Mississippi's Republican chairman, reminded the President that he could not have won in 1968 without his majorities in the Border South and said he could not expect to win again in 1972 without Southern votes.

It was to this turmoil that Mr. Nixon addressed himself at his press conference. He skipped the matter of tax exemption, leaving it to IRS to explain that it would be as patient and tolerant with applicant schools as the law allows. He had no intention, he said, "of sending vigilante squads, in effect, from the Justice Department, lawyers, in to coerce the Southern school districts to integrate. We have not done that; we are not going to do that. . . . Our policy . . . is cooperation without coercion." Senator Thurmond professed to take this statement to be a complete retreat, but it wasn't. Federal lawyers and other enforcers were still going into the South "to assist in achieving a smooth transition" from segregated to integrated schools and, although the White House and Justice Department minimized the fact, to receive and act upon complaints of fraudulent integration. The real policy was coerced cooperation where it could be obtained, enforced integration where no cooperation was to be found. Mr. Nixon, letting his grammar slip, foresaw in the coming Southern school year "a transition period which will be as least difficult as possible." His hope and his purpose are to get through that transition with his Southern Strategy intact and ready for 1972.

August 1, 1970

———

Senator Thurmond turned out to be less guillible than I had thought. Very few additional Federal enforcers were sent into the South. But persuasion and threats of positive enforcement were used to better effect than I had thought possible in July.

XXIV

A Very Good Day

"I have had a very good day," the President said toward the end of his Friday in New Orleans. Before the day was over, at a lush reception for Southern journalists, and afterward, winging home through the night aboard Air Force One, the assistants and Cabinet members who accompanied Mr. Nixon were asking reporters to agree that it was "a great day," "the best day we've had," and even, in a burst of euphoric exaggeration, the best and most important day for the cause of desegregation since the Supreme Court ruled in 1954 that the segregation of public schools by race violates the Constitution.

It was hardly that, but it was a good day for the President and incidentally for White House reporters who wonder on the more frequent and less rewarding days why grown men spend their time in the study of Richard Nixon. At the day's start, flying southward from Washington, the President let himself be truthful about his purpose. His declared purpose was to meet in New Orleans with the white chairmen and the black vice-chairmen of citizens' committees that had variously been formed and were still being formed in seven Southern states to promote public acceptance of school desegregation in the 700 or so districts where segregation in dual

systems persisted. Senator Allen Ellender of Louisiana remarked on the way down that he had some worries about being re-elected in 1972. "If I were as sure of '72 as you are," Mr. Nixon replied in the hearing of reporters, "I wouldn't be making this trip."

Outside the Royal Orleans Hotel in the French Quarter, after his passage by motorcade from the airport over highways and through streets lined with friendly Southerners, the President recalled that he and Mrs. Nixon first visited New Orleans in 1941 and thanked the crowd for its welcome to "somebody that was nothing, as I was 29 years ago." He thought it necessary to explain his presence on this day, in full entourage, in much the way that he had explained himself and his recent itch to be anywhere but Washington during visits to Fargo, North Dakota, Salt Lake City, Los Angeles, and Denver. "Instead of just sitting in Washington waiting for the people to come there," he said in New Orleans, "we are bringing the White House to all over the country. And now"—his voice rising to emphasize his point—"it is right here in Washington, D.C." We reporters laughed, but there was an edgy note in the laughter. In Denver, in a similarly exuberant moment before a similarly stimulating crowd, the President introduced John N. Mitchell as "the Attorney General of the United Nations" and, in a reference to the federal budget, he said thousands when he meant millions of dollars. In the course of a serious and obviously well-considered statement for reporters and television, he also said in Denver that Charles Manson, a defendant who was on trial for his life in Los Angeles, "was guilty, directly or indirectly, of eight murders without reason." Verbal slips, usually trivial, are nothing new for Mr. Nixon. But, one was entitled to reflect at that good and gay moment in New Orleans, they seemed to be occurring more often of late than they had in the recent past.

Mr. Nixon transacted his chief business in New Orleans with care and precision. There were no slips when he said to the national press and to the South, after his meeting with the white and black committeemen: "The highest court of the land has spoken. The unitary school system must replace the dual school system throughout the United States. The law having been determined, it is the responsibility of those in the federal government and particularly the responsibility of the President of the United States to uphold the law. And I shall meet that responsibility."

It was an interesting statement, skillfully framed, and its theme was the one that the President stressed again and again in private sessions, first with the full Louisiana committee (which had been pulled together in the previous 48 hours) and then at greater length with the 14 chairmen and vice chairmen. It was the Supreme Court, not Congress and not the President and the Nixon Administration, that was responsible for the law that Mr. Nixon now proposed to uphold and for the uncomfortable necessity for the South to complete, by the fall, the processes of formal desegregation. The imperative now was "orderly transition" from the last centers of "dual system" segregation to the minimal desegregation required to qualify the holdout districts as "unitary" school systems. With great earnestness, Mr. Nixon emphasized his overriding concern that "quality education" be maintained or, where it did not exist, be attained in public school systems. He never referred, on his own, to the all-white private schools to which thousands of white children were fleeing, and to his decision that they should be eligible for tax exemption only if they nominally agreed to admit non-whites. He similarly avoided any explicit statement of the measures he proposed to take to "uphold the law," preferring to emphasize instead his hope and his wish that compliance come about through Southern "cooperation" rather than by federal "coercion." The fact that most of the resistant school districts in the entire South were under some form of federal coercion, in the shape of court orders or the administrative termination of federal subsidies, was not mentioned.

Some of the community leaders, mostly bankers and lawyers and educators, who heard Mr. Nixon said afterward that they were impressed by his performance. Most of them had already had brief sessions with him in Washington, when their committees were formed in July and early August. The accounts they gave after the New Orleans meeting differed in detail from those given by the Nixon people, but not in ways that indicated any serious distortion. George B. Hall, the Alexandria lawyer who is chairman of the Louisiana committee, and his vice chairman, Jesse Stone, Jr., a black lawyer from Shreveport, said it was true that, as Nixon assistants had said, the atmosphere in the committee room was "hairy," with white and black men who mostly were meeting each other for the first time glaring at each other when Nixon subordinates and then the President himself appeared. Afterward, Hall and Stone said, there was at least a feeling among the committeemen that they might get together for a useful purpose, though they still didn't know just what they could do about the problems. The occasion, Hall said, "was as successful as a meeting can be in a fishbowl. Its hard to get a bunch of people together, in all the confusion, with the President arriving, and all." Jesse Stone, the black lawyer, said he told the President that black Louisianans, too, wanted "an orderly transition" toward "quality education," but they also wanted it "with justice"—meaning an end to the firing of black teachers, the closing of black schools, and "one way" desegregation that placed most of the burden and loss upon the blacks. "I don't know that it was necessary for me to say that to the President, but I did and he listened," Stone said.

Stone was asked whether the President had said at any point that he intended to uphold the law because the law was right. "I don't recall his saying that," Stone answered. "He did say, he intended to fulfill his responsibilities. But I don't recall his saying what the responsibilities were and how he intended to fulfill them." Even so, Stone thought the meetings and the President's presence were useful. "After all," he said, "the man who came in was the President of the United States. His presence and his statement probably made some of the people there more willing than they had been to address themselves to some of the easier questions." The hard questions, Stone said, were raised by him and others but were not discussed in any detail.

At the regional meeting, a committeeman showed Mr. Nixon the 100-page book of directions and the 25½-page questionnaire that applicant districts were required to digest and fill out in order to qualify for some of the $75 million in immediate emergency funds and perhaps $1.5 billion in later appropriations with which the Administration hopes to ease and hasten the President's "orderly transition." Big-city authorities might be able to handle such documents, the committeeman said, but smaller districts couldn't. Quietly furious, Mr. Nixon turned to HEW Secretary Elliot Richardson and ordered him to get the application form cut down to manageable length right away. Get that money out there, the President said, get it where it's needed. On the Monday following his Friday in New Orleans, a shorter form was submitted to Mr. Nixon and he approved it.

August 29, 1970

XXV

As He Was

San Clemente, California

Twice on August 29, at midday and in late afternoon, I put aside Jules Witcover's *The Resurrection of Richard Nixon* and went to see what the resurrected Nixon was letting his staff say about his doings on the second Saturday of his third stay in three months at the Western White House. There were no briefings by the President's press secretary over the weekend and the only information was in notices posted in our temporary press room, in a hotel twelve miles up the California coast from the Nixon compound. The day's two notices confirmed my hunch that I would learn more about Mr. Nixon from Witcover's account of him as he was during the six years before he acquired the protective mantle of the Presidency than I would from anything that he and his assistants volunteered about him now. We were told at noon: "The President spent the morning at his residence. He spent an hour and a half working in his study. There is no schedule to announce for the remainder of the day." And at 4:30 P.M.: "The President worked in the office for three hours. Later he relaxed around the residence with Mr.

Rebozo and Mr. Abplanalp and spent some time on the beach."
Any complaint that these sparse bulletins were wholly worthless
would be churlish and in error. It was to be expected, and therefore
interesting, that Mr. Nixon had once again summoned across the
continent his particular chums, Charles G. "Bebe" Rebozo and
Robert Abplanalp, both of whom are rich and discreet and, the
record of many years indicates, utterly subservient to and unde-
manding of their eminent friend. The references to the President at
work, at the seaside home he bought in 1969, and at his office on
the Coast Guard grounds adjoining it, reflected his and his staff's
anxiety, apparent all week, that the public not suppose for a moment that Mr. Nixon would be so indifferent to his duties as to
devote a single day entirely to rest after a run of arduous days. This
in itself was an intriguing departure from the pattern of the President's first stays at his California home and offices. Then he frequently golfed and lounged around his pool. His senior assistants
made a point of telling how their announced staff sessions with him
often consisted of leisurely conversational walks along the closed
and guarded beach in front of his home. Then the official supposition was that it was good for Mr. Nixon to be depicted and known
as a man who, for all of his tense earnestness, is capable of taking
his ease. In his second year in office the opposite assumption
seemed to prevail.

The same defensive quality, an aspect of the earlier Nixon that
pervades the Witcover portrait of him in the resurrection years,
marked his and his staff's handling of the public-relations problem
presented by the enormous logistical task involved in conducting
the Presidency in California. He and his spokesmen compounded
the problem for themselves. Instead of assuming that most people
would concede that what is good for a President is good for the
country, within reason, the Nixon spokesmen labored mightily to
create an impression that hauling coveys of ranking assistants and
advisers, the entire domestic Cabinet and supporting staffs from
Washington to California and back in government jets requires no
great effort or expenditure. Of course it does, a fact that was mag-
nified rather than minimized with the typical explanation that the
economic advisers flown out for one of the Nixon meetings were
merely three among 35 persons traveling in the same airplane to
serve the western Presidency in unidentified ways.

It was a rewarding pleasure to turn, at this time in this place,

from the screened Nixon of today to the Nixon recalled and revealed by Jules Witcover, who is rated by his colleagues among the
best of Washington's political reporters. His story begins on the
November morning in 1962 when Nixon knew that California
voters had denied him his home state's governorship in a defeat
that was far more humiliating than his narrow defeat for the Presidency in 1960 had been. Witcover has Nixon saying "Screw
them . . . Screw them" again and again to Herbert Klein, now his
Director of Communications, when Klein begs him to appear in
person before the reporters clamoring in a Los Angeles hotel for a
concession statement. Then he does appear, looking his worst on
television, "the small dark eyes, tight mouth, rubbery nose, and self-
conscious demeanor" presenting him "in his least photogenic, most
self-damaging aspect." There follows the famous tirade that Nixon
and everyone else then thought to be the end of his political career
—thanking the press, damning the press; thanking his campaign
workers for "a magnificent job" and damning them for an insufficient one; and saying in an excess of bitterness, "You won't have
Nixon to kick around any more because, gentlemen, this is my last
press conference. . . ." To this familiar event, ever worth recall,
Witcover adds two interesting points. Whatever drove Nixon to
that performance, it was not the shock of an unexpected defeat. He
expected it and coolly assured associates that he did before the
votes were counted. Nixon later persuaded himself that his outburst accounted for the kindlier treatment the press gave him in
subsequent years. He told Witcover in 1966 that the California
experience and the culminating press conference "served a purpose. The press had a guilt complex about their inaccuracy. Since
then, they have been generally accurate, and far more respectful."
    Nixon said this during an airborne interview that Witcover
judged afterward to be "either pure revelation or one of the great
put-ons of the year." Nixon really wanted to be a student, a
teacher, a writer: "I'd like to write two or three books a year, go to
one of the fine schools—Oxford, for instance—just teach, read and
write. I'd like to do that better than what I'm doing now. I don't
mean writing is easy for me, but writing phrases that move
people, that to me is something." Witcover perceived that Nixon
was doing what he was for a reason that fundamentally accounted
for his rise from the depths of 1962—his dedication to "the political life." Chance, calculation, ruthless skill, the rush of unpredict-

able events such as the Kennedy assassinations, the Vietnam war, the disastrous Goldwater candidacy in 1964, and Lyndon Johnson's withdrawal in 1968, had their parts in opening the way to the Presidency. But Nixon would not have been there to take the opened way if the political life did not attract him as it did and does. His law practice and the modest wealth it provided were valued incidentals. He once told an associate, who told Witcover, that he would be mentally dead in two years and physically dead in four if all he had to do was practice law.

No honest reporter can be wholly kind to Richard Nixon, and Witcover is not. Traveling on a 1966 campaign trip with Nixon, "At times it suddenly struck me that the man never seemed, even in a crowded room, to be really with anybody—and that he preferred it that way." Nixon's penchant for trying "to milk every possible political advantage from a situation, and yet to back off when its implications were laid out before him, made him very transparent at times. He seemed to realize that some observers were aware of this tactic, and to be embarrassed by that fact." Hence the beseeching smiles, the flickers of visible pain, the awkward attempts at recovery when he senses that he has repelled people whom he essentially doesn't give a damn about.

Yet this is a fair book, crediting Nixon with more than some may think he deserves for his sense of organization, his endurance, his appeal to the many people who do not share the usual reporter's tendency to look for flaws and enjoy dwelling upon them. This being so, the reaction to the book at the Nixon White House when Witcover was researching it last year and since it appeared is revealing. It is said for Nixon that he hasn't read it and doesn't intend to. Witcover got the official freeze when he told the press staff that he was going to write the book, and there still is a discernible chill when it is mentioned in that quarter. Nixon associates who confess that they have read it have been pleasantly surprised when they find that it isn't a hatchet job. Jules Witcover is not a hatcheteer, but that matters little to the Nixon people. They prefer safely and soundly committed writers—committed, that is, to Richard Nixon. One of the crosses that Mr. Nixon and his staff apologists have to bear is that there are so few reporters and writers around with the preferred qualifications.

September 5, 1970

XXVI

Agnew
on the Road

San Clemente, California

The Nixon staff managed to make Vice President Agnew's public accounting of his second Asian trip an absurd and laughable prelude to the political campaigning that he was about to embark upon. The absurdity was not intended, of course. The intention was to show Mr. Agnew to the best possible advantage as a sedate, distinguished, and freshly informed statesman, summoned to the Western White House from Honolulu a day earlier than he had expected, in order to share with the President and assembled policy advisers not only the Vice President's findings in South Korea, Taiwan, South Vietnam, Cambodia, and Thailand, but the wisdom and views that he might contribute to the handling of the difficulties that endangered the negotiation of a settlement between Israel and its Arab enemies in the Middle East.

"WITH ENEMIES LIKE SPIRO, WHO NEEDS FRIENDS?"

When the Vice President left San Clemente for Asia on August 22, the President appeared with him on the photogenic knoll that lies between the Nixon office and the Pacific Ocean and then, in company with Secretary of State William P. Rogers and staff adviser Henry Kissinger, saw the traveler into the gleaming Marine helicopter that ferried him to a Presidential jet. Mr. Agnew said at the time that he was being sent to Asia to tell his official hosts what they "know very well"—namely, that under the Nixon Doctrine the United States proposes from now on to maintain its presence in the Far East at decreasing cost to itself and at increasing cost to its allies and proteges. By his account during the trip and at San Clemente when he returned, that is all that he accomplished. Reporters who accompanied him and resident American officials along the way agreed that he did it gracefully, the while he generated satisfactory headlines and televised glimpses of Agnew expounding and selling Nixon policy as it had been thoroughly explained to him before he left. Some flurried reporting to the contrary notwithstanding, he added nothing to the policy and subtracted nothing from it.

A different show was planned for his return and it almost came off. First there was a photographed session in the President's office. Mr. Nixon handed Mr. Agnew a golf ball adorned with the Presidential seal, told him to use it "for putting only," and admonished him to get a good rest before taking the jet trail in behalf of Republican candidates for Congress this fall. Only Press Secretary Ronald Ziegler, looking as if he knew that something silly was coming up, walked out with the Vice President for the climactic display. Microphones and television cameras were set up in front of the office compound, angled so that the cameras commanded a clear view of the path to a Marine chopper in the background, some 200 feet away. Newspaper cameramen and reporters were ordered to stay where they were confined in a roped area when the Vice President finished speaking his piece. It was essential, a White House staff man said, that the television cameras have an unobstructed shot of the Vice President's receding back as he walked across an intervening expanse of grass and pavement to his helicopter. Mr. Agnew with his trim and erect figure, the noble head slightly marred by squinty eyes, in a dark suit and grey tie, his hands primly fixed at the hem of his jacket, was appropriately impressive when he said into the microphones that his trip had been worthwhile for him, the President, and the countries he visited. I don't know how the concluding walk came over the home screen, but to the watching press it was extremely funny, a welcomed and heartily ridiculed break in the solemnity that usually shrouds the Nixon White House. It was farce of a sort that had to be seen on the spot to be appreciated: the confessed contrivance, the cadenced pace of the Vice President, the pause at the foot of the chopper steps, and then the takeoff for a nearby hotel, where Mr. Agnew spent the afternoon and night, isolated from the press and in no further communication with Mr. Nixon.

Adequate communication between the President and his Vice President during the fall campaign operation has been elaborately assured, however casual and indirect and flattering to Mr. Agnew it will be made to seem. No piece of recent White House business had been accorded more serious attention by Mr. Nixon and his principal domestic assistants and advisers. Four of these gentlemen—H. R. Haldeman, John Ehrlichman, Bryce Harlow, and Robert Finch, with occasional assists from Budget Director George Shultz and OEO Director Donald Rumsfeld—participated with Mr. Nixon in extensive discussions of how best to capitalize for the Administration and for the Republican Party upon Mr. Agnew's standing with what all concerned take to be the core majority of American voters. The prime objective is to bring his identification with public order and with all that may be required to preserve it in a disorderly time to bear, with maximum effect, upon the effort to secure a Republican majority in the Senate at the November elections. The word at the White House is: watch where Agnew goes, first in the West and then through the country at large, and you will know where the Nixon political command figures that its best chances are. His second visit to Asia, planned since early June and foreseen since he completed the first one in January, was calculated to give the Vice President additional stature and at the same time to identify him in the public mind as Richard Nixon's emissary and subordinate—an esteemed personage and valued political property in his own right, but one who is required and willing to keep within the limits of policy and expression prescribed for him by the President.

Nobody at the White House, Agnew included, will acknowledge that the latter consideration has been a specific factor in the plans for his congressional campaign or that its concomitant, a latent apprehension that the Vice President may have gotten too big for his britches, is responsible in part for the unprecedented White House staff support that the President has provided him. When I mentioned the swelling Agnew britches to a trusted Nixon assistant in San Clemente, the response was wonderful to hear. No other Vice President in history, I was told, has enjoyed the confidence and received the support that Mr. Nixon has extended to Mr. Agnew. If Mr. Nixon thought it necessary to curb Mr. Agnew's exuberant tendencies, recently subdued, or to correct any impression that the Vice President has made himself independent of the President, somebody from the White House staff like John Ehrlichman or Robert Finch would have been assigned to oversee his campaign activities. Instead, the President had assigned to the Agnew campaign staff Counselor Bryce N. Harlow, economist Martin Anderson, and writer Patrick Buchanan, three Presidential assistants who are known to be in general sympathy with the Vice President's conservative views if not invariably with his customary way of expressing them. William Safire, another Nixon writer who has been ordered to provide intermittent assistance, was not mentioned in this connection, but he might as well have been.

The offered explanation and disavowal of concern omitted several pertinent facts. Counselor Finch is in overall charge of the campaign for Mr. Nixon, with a powerful say in the tone to be struck and in the dispatch of Administration speakers. Counselor Harlow, the temporary Agnew chief of staff, numbers among his assets a sharp eye for verbal boo-boos of the kind to which Agnew on his own is prone. Although he had drafted some of the most abrasive Agnew speeches, Pat Buchanan was among the first to advise the President, through senior intermediaries, that the Vice President's sometime references to impudent snobs, criminal activists, and the like had become counter-productive and should be discouraged.

The foregoing were among the thoughts that came to me when I watched the Vice President marching into the bright noon at San Clemente. Laughing, I reminded myself that Spiro T. Agnew is not a man to be laughed at, now or ever. Mr. Nixon was not laughing when he told a CBS television interviewer out here that the question whether Agnew will be on the Republican ticket in 1972 is premature.

September 19, 1970

"I'M LIGHTING MY WAY OUT OF THE JUNGLE."

XXVII

Vietnam Cooker

The President's Vietnam cooker is at work again in late September. What's cooking may be nothing more than a touched-up serving of the same old mess of Nixon peace pottage, but I persist in crediting Mr. Nixon with sense enough to know that something more and better than that will have to be produced before the mid-term November elections if his Vietnam policy is to be an asset rather than a liability to the Republican candidates, particularly for the Senate, in whose behalf he is using the power and prestige of the Presidency to the fullest possible extent.

That is what the President's long-planned and suddenly announced trip to Southern Europe is all about. He and his in-house political advisers, notably Counselor Robert Finch, concluded many weeks earlier that a show of Presidential movement and initiative abroad, in an area far removed from the Vietnam swamp, would be the best kind of campaigning that he could do at this stage for the Republican cause. They did not anticipate when the trip was planned that the vaunted Nixon peace initiative in the Middle East would be near collapse, but the unhappy circumstances could be turned to political account with the demonstration of Presidential and national concern Mr. Nixon's presence in the Mediterranean would constitute.

One would think from the official announcement of the President's itinerary and purposes that the Vietnam war and the end to it that Mr. Nixon keeps promising figure very little in his immediate business. "At some point on the trip," it was said in a noticeably casual fashion, the President would meet with Ambassadors David K. E. Bruce and Philip Habib, his chief negotiators at the abortive Paris peace talks. Where they would meet had not been determined, except that it would not be in Paris. Perhaps in Yugoslavia, where Mr. Nixon is to confer with President Tito on ways to further "peace and order in the world"? Maybe, but that hadn't been decided, either. "Don't let that spook you," a Nixon spokesman said when he was asked whether the elaborate effort to play down the Vietnam aspect of the trip hid something more than we were told. It didn't spook me, but it did inspire me to indulge in a little addition—a little exercise in putting two and three and four together—that I usually avoid in attempting to fathom this unpredictable President.

It was announced as a seeming afterthought, a footnote to the disclosure of the President's European journey, that Mr. Nixon had sent his chief domestic assistants and advisers, John Ehrlichman and George Shultz, off to South Vietnam, Japan, and Hongkong on a trip that would keep them away from Washington through September. They were being sent, it was said, to study for the President "the postwar situation" that will confront the US in South Vietnam, presumably meaning chiefly the economic burden that the United States will have to bear in South Vietnam when and if "a postwar situation" develops there. The stated excuses for the later stops in Japan and Hongkong were transparently fragile: to look into Japan's phenomenal economic recovery since World War II, and into public housing projects in Hongkong that the White House spokesman said he had never heard of until Ehrlichman told him to give that as one reason for the trip.

Sending Ehrlichman and Shultz on such a mission was an extraordinary thing to do, and it was done at an extraordinary time. Ehrlichman, the President's Assistant for Domestic Affairs, has been deeply engaged in setting up the new Domestic Council of Cabinet members and the policy staff that is supposed to serve it and the President. It is a job that is far from finished, and one on which the President's earnest quest for intelligent policy choices and decisions largely depends. George Shultz, who doubles as a very senior personal assistant to the President and as the director of the new Office of Management and Budget, had been worked into a state of nightly exhaustion in his endeavor to restructure the old Bureau of the Budget and to assume, through it and with his small personal staff, many of the operational duties that formerly fell to Ehrlichman and his staff. That job, too, is far from finished, and I decline to believe that Shultz has been diverted from it to "the postwar situation" in South Vietnam for no better reason than that this is as good a time as any to evaluate economic and political problems that have long since been studied and evaluated in stupendous detail.

In the course of a White House briefing for the press on Mr. Nixon's hopes that Congress can be persuaded to junk the present foreign-aid program and substitute for it a new combination of direct bilateral assistance and aid fed through international loan agencies, it was disclosed that the Administration had figured out a way—Congress willing—to increase aid to South Vietnam, Cambodia, and Indochina as a whole without identifying the program with the Vietnam war. The idea is to regard Southeast Asia as a single regional entity, leaving to the President the allocation to its individual countries of grants and loans authorized for the region. This seems quite sensible and, if adopted by Congress, it could be a means of assuring to South Vietnam and Cambodia in particular support on a scale that might encourage their respective governments to go along with political terms for settlement of the Vietnam-Indochina war that otherwise would never be acceptable to them. When a reporter asked the White House briefer whether it was true that economic aid to Cambodia alone under this scheme might come to a billion dollars, the official said with a guttural laugh that the reporter was talking in terms considerably more extravagant than those being seriously considered by the President's planners. It was the kind of reply that, if repeated in the proper quarters, might cause even President Thieu in Saigon to reconsider his opposition to anything approaching practical political terms for a settlement.

A speech that Ambassador Ellsworth Bunker delivered in Saigon

on September 14 could be further evidence that something is up—
something, conceivably, that the Ambassador doesn't much like.
He has stood throughout his tenure in Saigon for sturdy and un-
qualified American support of President Thieu, at the cost if necessary of prolonging the war until it can be ended on Thieu's terms—
which is to say, not really ended at all. The alternative is to end it
by negotiation, as Mr. Nixon has been saying since May of 1969
that he wants to end it and as I continue to believe he does. That
can be done only by proposing terms for negotiations that promise
Hanoi and the South Vietnamese Liberation Front some place in a
negotiated postwar government. Despite all of his talk about
ending the war only "in a way that contributes to a just and lasting
peace in Vietnam and in the world," the President has never re-
tracted his implied undertaking to negotiate such a settlement if
Hanoi will agree to negotiate at all. The invasion of Cambodia and
the President's subsequent toughened line of talk make it sadly difficult to remember and believe what has just been stated, but it remains true and Ambassador Bunker must know that it is true. The
prospect that some renewed effort to make it obviously true is on
Mr. Nixon's Vietnam cooker could have been on the Ambassador's
mind when he deemed it necessary to say to his Vietnamese audience: "We stand steadfastly beside you. You need not fear, and
Hanoi has no basis to hope, that our commitment has weakened. It
has not and will not. If we ever hope to move from an era of confrontation to an era of negotiation we must demonstrate now—at
this point where the Communist idea of confrontation is being
tested—that confrontation with the United States and its allies is
costly and unrewarding."

Somebody at the American Embassy in Saigon told the *Los
Angeles Times* correspondent who reported the speech that it "was
not cleared by the White House." The language suggests to me that
it was addressed to the White House. The Ambassador's speech
reads singularly like a lecture to Mr. Nixon, the author of the
phrase about moving "from an era of confrontation to an era of
negotiation."

Let this exercise in speculative addition end with a small fact
that may also be meaningless but that has interested me. Henry A.
Kissinger, the President's foreign policy man and the co-author of
his Vietnam policy, has been all but inaccessible of late to reporters
who usually find him quite accessible. Something is up that he

doesn't want to risk talking about. It could be something to do with the Middle East, but I think it's Vietnam.

September 26, 1970

———

At the end of October, four weeks after the foregoing was written, Mr. Nixon produced his revised proposals for settlement of the Vietnam-Indochina war. They turned out to be "the same old mess of Nixon peace pottage," somewhat touched up.

XXVIII

White House Staff

It looks as if the President, after 19 months of incessant fiddling with his staff structure, has evolved a setup that suits him well enough to see him through the remainder of his present term. One senses among his key people a feeling, new to the Nixon White House, that they know where they are now, with him and in terms of what he expects them to do for him. Odd though the observation may seem at a time of crisis and of collapsing hope and policy in the Middle East, the President and his assistants convey an appearance of orderly processes at work in an orderly way that is probably closer to the reality than skeptics like myself had believed possible. Whether this result, to the extent that it is real and not illusory, is as important to the country as it is to Mr. Nixon is an open question. But it is of at least middling importance that a President have at hand the administrative means to do his job in the way he thinks best for him.

An interesting paradox is apparent in Mr. Nixon's use of the structure to which he has devoted so much of his time and energy. Having fitted his principal assistants into neat organizational boxes, each bounded by precisely defined lines of responsibility, he is forever jerking them out of their assigned roles and giving them special jobs. George P. Shultz, the director of the new Office of Management and Budget, counts himself lucky when he is able to sit through a weekly meeting of that agency's enlarged executive staff without being summoned to the President's office for consultation on matters that may range from budgetary policy to school desegregation. John D. Ehrlichman, the assistant for domestic affairs and executive director of the Cabinet-level Domestic Council, is supposed in theory to confine himself and his staff to the formulation of domestic policy proposals, and leave the execution of adopted policy to Shultz and OMB. But it doesn't work out that way, mainly because the President won't let it. Ehrlichman is deep in operations, Shultz in policy making. Both of them spent two weeks of September in the Far East, roving in the President's behalf from South Vietnam to Japan and Hong Kong. Donald Rumsfeld, who is both an assistant to the President and director of the Office of Economic Opportunity, has conducted a study of federal grants to cities, participated in the planning for the Republican congressional campaign, worked on a review of national domestic priorities and, along with these and other assigned chores, supervised a reorganization of OEO aimed at making it less disruptive of the established order than it had become under the Democrats. Former HEW Secretary Robert Finch, now a staff counselor with Cabinet status, said that "It's great, just great, to be a Cabinet member without having to run a big department. I'm in on everything." He had a hand in managing the congressional campaign for the President, worked with Ehrlichman and others on school desegregation, and kept in uneasy touch with the Scranton commission on campus unrest.

The test of the Nixon structure is what comes from it. When I asked in August for an example of what the new Domestic Council had accomplished in the three months since it was established, with the promise that it would be the domestic equivalent of the National Security Council, I was told to await a forthcoming reexamination of the Model Cities program. This is the program, lodged in the Department of Housing and Urban Development, that is intended to concentrate federal money and energies upon the rehabilitation of blighted urban areas. Five Cabinet members of the Council, their staffs, and several of Ehrlichman's White House assistants devoted many meetings and countless man-hours to a review of the program. Ehrlichman thought in mid-August that the resulting report was ready for release, but it was still in the works in late September. Its intended thrust is clear: the federal government must somehow find a way to require the effective spending of federal money for local purposes without depriving local authorities of creative autonomy and initiative. A Presidential task force came to the same conclusion months before the Domestic Council was established, and Nixon assistants were saying the same thing on their own before the task force was appointed. The utmost claimed for the Council report, when it finally appears, is that it will suggest some trial-and-error ways to reconcile federal responsibility with local responsibility and insights. That may justify the enormous effort that has gone into the study and report, but even Mr. Nixon must reflect at times upon the disparity between his kind of structured effort and real accomplishment.

Director Shultz has said that the new Office of Management and Budget, replacing the former Bureau of the Budget, embodies "a sharply concentrated and significantly strengthened effort to assist the President in the development and management of federal programs." It is intended to be the President's principal instrument of command, extending and strengthening his control over the entire federal establishment and especially over the domestic departments and agencies. The OMB formally evolved from the recommendations of a study commission headed by the President's friend, Roy Ash of Litton Industries, but its origins may be traced also to the irritation of Mr. Nixon and some of his assistants, notably John Ehrlichman, with the old Bureau of the Budget as they found it working when they took office. It seemed to them that the Budget Bureau's career economists, program analysts, and statisticians had their heads buried in their own expertise, serving more often to frustrate than to further Presidential aims. It was the unfair reaction of men, many of them newcomers to government, who knew more about what they wanted to do than how to do it, but their angers and resentments contributed materially to the President's decision to establish the OMB and bring former Labor Secretary Shultz to the White House to head it.

If organization will solve or substantially help to solve a President's problems, the OMB should be all that Mr. Nixon intends it to be. Shultz, in his dual role as OMB director and a personal assistant to the President, working from the West Wing of the White House, has the clout to make the new system work if anyone can. His standing with the President is such that no other assistant dares or cares to cross either him or his OMB subordinates, who are encouraged now to think of themselves as members rather than monitors of the White House staff. Caspar Weinberger, a San Francisco lawyer who served briefly as chairman of the Federal Trade Commission, is deputy director in charge of the detailed budgetary process. Associate Director Arnold Weber oversees five reorganized and consolidated bureau divisions charged with improving the management of federal activities throughout government. Three noncareer assistant directors, political appointees but also highly professional technicians in their respective fields, are taking over the responsibility not only for the budgets of all departments and agencies but for their working relationships and communication with the White House and the Presidential staff. Shultz has told them and the heads of the concerned departments and agencies that he expects the assistant directors to be his and the President's "desk men," in effect the White House assistants to whom department and agency heads turn first when they have business with the President or with Mr. Nixon's own assistants.

This will take some doing. Richard Nathan, Donald Rice, and James R. Schlesinger, the assistant directors in question, are in fact assistants to Shultz, not Nixon, and no amount of persuasion to the contrary is likely to assuage the doubts of Cabinet-rank department heads who prefer to believe that they are the President's men. Elaborate efforts to identify the assistant OMB directors with the President, through Shultz, are in train and they may work out to better effect than is suggested here. But they overlook a small point that has not occurred to the President's management experts. A Cabinet member who wants to telephone Nathan, Rice, or Schlesinger will not find any of them at the White House number (456–1414). They are on the Executive Office line (395–3000). A change of telephone numbers might be helpful.

October 3, 1970

———

The Model Cities report never did appear. A week after the foregoing was published, Assistant Directors Nathan, Rice, and Schlesinger were placed on the White House telephone line.

XXIX

With Dick
in Europe

Limerick, Ireland

Mr. Nixon offered the best possible commentary upon his latest
trip to Europe—the third of his Presidency if his stops in Rumania
and Britain at the end of his Asian tour last year are counted—
when he volunteered to help the reporters who accompanied him
make a degree of sense out of this journey that the honest ones
among us could not pretend to make on our own. By the time we
arrived here after visits in six days to Italy, the Vatican, the Sixth
Fleet in the Mediterranean, Yugoslavia, Spain, and Britain, the accepted wisdom in the press party was that the trip made no coherent sense and had produced no discernible pattern of purpose
and accomplishment. It had amounted, we told each other, to little
more than cumulative and wearying confirmation of the fact that it
was conceived for domestic political purposes and of the prospect

that it was soon to be exploited to the full for those purposes in the last weeks of the congressional compaign. The President's press secretary, Ronald Ziegler, was so informed when he asked some of the frustrated correspondents in his charge what they thought of the expedition. William Safire, a Nixon writer who was abruptly detached from campaign duty with Vice President Agnew and flown here to assist the President in preparing something believable and useful to say when he got home, wandered among his journalist friends at the bar of the Limerick Inn, asking with rather forlorn mockery whether they had discovered "a great, underlying theme" in the trip and, if so, would they please tell him what it was. He was told and presumably reported to Mr. Nixon that the traveling press was fresh out of great, underlying themes.

The President sought to repair the lack in a 20-minute discourse to reporters whom he invited to a cocktail party on Sunday afternoon at a hotel that used to be an Irish castle. He came to his party from Kilfrush House, one of two Irish mansions owned by his host for the weekend, John A. Mulcahy, a multi-millionaire Irish-American manufacturer who is said to contribute generously to the Republican Party, to various Catholic and conservative causes, and to the economy of this part of Ireland. Mr. Nixon had intended to spend the afternoon and night at the second Mulcahy mansion, which is reputed to be even bigger and more lavishly refurbished than Kilfrush House, an edifice that reminded reporters who saw it and its surrounding 225 acres of a miniature Hilton hotel. Army Signal Corps switchboards complete with operators, technicians, and miles of secured telephone lines had been set up at both places, and the one at the second mansion was quietly dismantled when Mr. Nixon changed his mind. It was an unnoticed casualty, pica-yune in relative cost, of the enormous logistical operation that must attend a Presidential tour. Mr. Nixon said at his party that he worked through the afternoon on White House chores—including, his guests gathered from what he also said, the careful preparation of "some conclusions with regard to the trip" that he hoped the press would find helpful.

His conclusions were interesting in themselves, but they were even more interesting for what they and the way in which they were presented revealed of Mr. Nixon. Some of the reporters who were there (I was down with a cold and rely here upon their impressions) perceived beneath his appearance of genial ease a strained and conscious attempt at self-control. The official transcript bears out that impression. It was evident that Mr. Nixon not only wanted the press to accept and be guided by his conclusions but had persuaded himself that they amounted to a correct and sufficient explanation and justification. His earnest tone and manner left no doubt about that. But something, perhaps a doubt that the reporters would be as impressed by his account as he was, bothered him. His hands, clasped firmly to the front, flew out occasionally in that nervous, beseeching way of his. Twice (some said three times) he said "Sixth Feet" when he meant "Sixth Fleet." He got the sequence of his recent travels wrong: "That is why I first visited the Sixth Fleet," he said, forgetting that he had first visited President Saragat of Italy and Pope Paul. He stumbled painfully when he spoke of "irresponsible, radical elements" in the Middle East that could "set in the course of events, the train of events, set in motion —I meant to say—a train of events that would escalate into a possible confrontation between major powers in the area."

The Nixon conclusions may be summarized as follows. His purpose—"*the* purpose"—was "to strengthen the structure of peace" and to strengthen it particularly "in the Mediterranean area." For this he relied upon NATO, upon such allies as Italy and Greece, but especially upon the US Sixth Fleet and the "military stability and military strength" that it embodied. Friendship for the United States, understanding if not total support of its policies among the leaders of nonaligned nations, confidence in the American desire and will for peace in Vietnam and elsewhere—these were important, and he felt that he had contributed to all these factors with his trip. But his great, underlying theme, the one that the President emphasized on this occasion and throughout the trip, was the importance and necessity of sustained American military power and his special determination to sustain that power as it was represented by the Sixth Fleet in the Mediterranean and Middle Eastern areas.

Mr. Nixon, in short, was off on a power kick. He had convinced himself, and now sought to convince others, that the American power vested in the Sixth Fleet and its deterrent effect primarily accounted for the recent resolution of the conflict in Jordan. The most that one of his closest foreign policy advisers had previously claimed and still claimed was that the US made "a significant contribution" to the containment of the Jordanian crisis. Others gave more credit to Soviet persuasion and the Israeli forces massed at Jordan's borders. Mr. Nixon was having none of that sort of humility when and after he arrived in Rome. His own words justify the statement that he was imbued to the point of obsession with American power and with the power of the American Presidency.

At the end of his Vatican audience, he reminded Pope Paul that the President of the United States was about to take off in an Army helicopter from St. Peter's Square to visit "the mightiest military force which exists in the world on any ocean." He walked from the Papal Library into the Vatican's Clementine Room and said to American clerics assembled there that "the power of the spirit" which they exercise fills a need "that can't be filled by a man even as powerful as the President of the United States." He also said, with questionable accuracy, that he was about to visit "the mightiest fleet that has ever been assembled in the history of the world," and concluded with these words: "Speaking very humbly, as President of the strongest nation in the world, with more power, perhaps, than any leader in the world, I can say with all the power I have, you have something, you and your colleagues, that the world needs and particularly the young people of the world need very much today." He told the same hearers a little story about himself. Sometimes in the night at the White House, he said, he comes half awake and thinks of a problem that he ought to speak to the President about. "Then, when I am fully awake, I realize that I am the President."

It seemed for awhile that the shock of Gamel Nasser's death, with its unpredictable effects upon the Nixon search for peace in the Middle East, and the eight hours the President spent with Josip Tito in Yugoslavia, had served to moderate the power rhetoric. Nixon and Tito appeared to hit it off impressively well and I am in no position to disagree with correspondents who concluded, partly for want of any more satisfying conclusion, that the exposure to Marshal Tito's view of the world may turn out to have been the one really productive aspect of the trip. But it must be noted that Mr. Nixon was still pondering the news of Nasser when he assured the men of the Sixth Fleet that "the fact that we were ready with the power exemplified by this mighty fleet" constituted "the most important, indispensable reason" why general war had not erupted in the Middle East. In his summation for the press in Ireland, the

President attached more importance to what he considered to have been his success in bringing Marshal Tito to an adequate understanding of American policy than to any new understanding that he, Mr. Nixon, may have derived from his Yugoslav host. One of Tito's beliefs, politely expressed to Mr. Nixon, is that the United States and the Soviet Union could best serve the interests of the Mediterranean area by getting out of it. Mr. Nixon was talking about and to the Soviet Union when he said in Ireland: ". . . in the event that other forces, naval forces, should threaten the position of strength which the Sixth Fleet now enjoys, then the United States must be prepared to take the action necessary to maintain that overall strength of the Sixth Fleet." He was not asked and he did not attempt to reconcile this assertion with the substantial reductions of American naval and other military power, Vietnam apart, to which he is committed.

The President's only assay at serious business in Ireland, at the end of his trip, was a Sunday morning conference at Kilfrush House with Ambassadors David K. E. Bruce and Philip Habib, his negotiators at the Vietnam talks in Paris. Mr. Nixon forbade his spokesmen and companions, Henry Kissinger included, to say one meaningful word about the meeting and its possible consequences in the way of a fresh Vietnam initiative. He reserved any announcement along that line for himself and he is welcome to the privilege. After watching and hearing Mr. Nixon on his power jag in Europe, I will believe that he is capable of a true peace initiative in Vietnam when he proves it.

October 17, 1970

It turned out that Safire was summoned to Europe to draft the speech setting forth Mr. Nixon's October "peace proposals." H. R. Haldeman, the President's staff chief, told several reporters and Press Secretary Ronald Ziegler that my report of the European trip was "the shittiest piece of journalism I ever saw."

XXX

America's Mission

Herewith I offer an account of Mr. Nixon's view of the world and of what he conceives to be the American mission in the world as of 1970 and perhaps for the next 25 years. Its simple banalities are not mine, nor can they be attributed directly to the President. But they are stated in terms that he would use in a more polished form and in the first person if he were speaking for the record. In Mr. Nixon's view:

His reputation for being a very strong anti-Communist is correct and it is pleasing. It is pleasing because he continues to regard himself as a very strong anti-Communist. His dislike of Communism increases when he visits Communist countries. The grayness of life and thought and expression that he observes in those countries confirms him in his preference for free societies and in his dislike of Communism.

But he as President knows that he must look at the Communists' side of it. They don't like our system any more than he likes theirs. If we are to comprehend and cope with their view of the world, we have to realize that the differences between the United States and the Soviet Union are so deep and so profound that they are not going to be resolved by smiles, handshakes, summit conferences between the top leaders. It is not true that the real divisions between the US and the Soviet Union have been exaggerated, that it is simply a question of our not understanding them and their not understanding us. They understand us. Perhaps we understand them better than we used to. If we start with the fundamental proposition (simple as it sounds, this proposition is of enormous importance to Mr. Nixon) that we are different and that we are competitors and that we are going to continue to be competitors as long as this generation lives, then we can have a sound basis for a meaningful settlement of the major differences.

For example, the Russians differ with the Americans with regard to a settlement in Vietnam. They differ because they would prefer to see the Communists prevail in South Vietnam. (The corollary that the United States would prefer to see the non-Communists prevail is implied but not stated.) That does not mean, however, that the United States and the Soviet Union will allow their differences over Vietnam to drag the two powers into a major confrontation.

A more important, a vitally important, area of difference is the Middle East. There the Soviet Union wants and in the past ten years has made tremendous strides toward gaining an opening to Africa, an opening into the Mediterranean. They want to turn the southern hinge of NATO. There we, the United States, want to deny any expansionist power domination of that critical area of the world. Even in this vitally important area of vital differences, however, the outcome of the recent Jordanian crisis indicated that when the chips are really down neither the Soviet Union nor the United States will allow itself to be dragged into a major confrontation leading to war. (Whether the chips were really down during the Jordan affair is disputed in Washington, but Mr. Nixon likes to have it believed that they were.)

Now we come to the blue chip—Europe and NATO. NATO was set up (in 1949) for several reasons: Western Europe's postwar weakness, its and our fear of the Soviet Union, but also for a third and very important reason—to find a home for the West Germans. Germany is still the heart of the problem in Europe, and the Soviet Union's ideas about Germany and the future of NATO are diametrically opposed to ours. But, here again, the question is, do we allow the differences to draw the two powers into a major confrontation? Probably not, because there are great elements working against a confrontation. Everyone in the President's official family agrees that these elements are the following, in order of importance: first, neither major power is likely to make the kind of decision that would lead to the nuclear obliteration of 40- to 70-million people in each country; second, the Soviet Union with its smaller gross national product has an even greater interest than the United States has in stopping the rise of defense expenditures; and third, both countries have an interest in increasing trade with each other. So there they are, the great elements working against confrontation: avoid war, reduce defense expenditures, trade.

Finally we come to the role that the United States should play. Many Americans, not a majority but a very substantial number, are very tired of America's playing an international role. They want to get out of Vietnam; they want to bring the troops home from Europe; they don't want to be involved any place in the world. The old internationalists, many of them, have turned isolationist because of the same motivation that made them internationalists in the first place: a feeling of compassion for downtrodden people around the world now makes them nationalists, turning inward at this time, looking at the problems at home and saying: *Away with the problems of the world. We haven't been able to do much about them. Let's turn homeward.*

Who would have thought, at the end if World War II, that the United States would be first, the Soviet Union second, Japan third, and Germany fourth among the world's powers? Yet this has happened. In the next 25 years, Japan, now a major power, may become a military power. Certainly China will become a major power. So over the next 25 years there may be five great power centers—Japan, China, a unified Europe, the Soviet Union, and the United States. What Americans must realize is very simply this: if the United States is going to the sidelines, there are going to be only two major contestants left on the field. One will be the Soviet Union and the other will be Communist China, moving up. Americans must recognize that there is no other nation in the free world that can play a role—play a role, not to defeat the Soviet Union or Communist China, but at least to be a counterbalance against the expansionist efforts of Communist China and the Soviet Union in the years ahead.

With all of its faults, the United States in this century has had as its goal not expansion but simply the defense of freedom and independence around the world. Americans can be very proud of that fact. The reason that small nations· are petrified at the thought of the United States turning away from its world responsibilities is that they know that the United States in a world role will respect their independence. No nation—*no nation*—fears that the United States will compromise its independence or dominate it. When this is said, the reference is not to the views of publicists and intellectuals, so-called, but to national leaders—Tito and the rest. This cannot be said of the two other major powers in the world, the Soviet Union and Communist China. That is why the United States' role is so important to the world. If Americans retreat to the sidelines, they will leave the field to those who do have a great thrust of power, and who would move onward to expand their role wherever they possibly could.

This finally comes down to whether the United States can do it or not. That is really a question of leadership at the national level. But it is also a question of leadership in the nation's universities, in its intellectual community, in the press, in television. This Administration does not want unanimity of opinion. But it is important that the United States continue in the next 25 years the free world leadership that it still has. Whether Americans can and will do it depends upon whether they have the understanding, the stamina, the patience, the wisdom, the character to see it through.

October 24, 1970

———

A writer in the *Washington Post* of November 28, 1970, reported that a similar summary of Mr. Nixon's views was derived "from a Nixon backgrounder to a group of editors." Under White House rules, I was not free to say as much when the foregoing paraphrase was prepared or to connect it with "background" remarks which the President made to a group of editors at Hartford, Connecticut, on October 12.

XXXI

Now Do It!

The President's last stop on his first day of open campaigning for Republican candidates was at Green Bay, Wisconsin. It was early evening and the weather was mild, a welcome change after a day of political labor on windswept airports and in cold hangars in Vermont, New Jersey, and Pennsylvania. Perhaps a thousand people stood at the edge of the Green Bay airport, behind local and state policemen and banks of portable floodlights. The lights were focused upon Air Force One, the blue and cream Presidential jet, leaving the crowd obscured in the dusk. Mr. Nixon, after a brief initial appearance, was aboard the plane, in conference with John Erickson, the Republican opponent of Democratic Senator William Proxmire; Lieutenant Governor Jack Olson, the candidate for Governor; and Congressman John Byrnes, up for reelection to his fourteenth term. Most of the people outside were friendly. A hundred or so of them were not. They were young, they were clustered in a group to the right of Air Force One, and they were interspersing calls for "Peace Now" and "End the War" with ritual chants that the President and his companions had heard at Burlington in Vermont, at Teterboro in New Jersey, at Lancaster in Pennsylvania: "One-two-three-four—we don't like your fucking war" and "Five-six-seven-eight—we don't want a fascist state."

One of the chanters, a girl in blue jeans, fascinated me with her display of an unusual talent. She was chewing gum, and she never stopped chewing while she chanted. Two boys in their late teens, also chanting but not chewing, stood behind her. I went up to them and asked them if they realized that they and their friends were being extremely stupid and doing Mr. Nixon an enormous favor. The girl and the two boys fell silent for a moment, staring, and the girl actually stopped chewing. After the pause she said, "Sure, we realize it," and resumed her chanting and chewing. Baffled, I stepped back and found myself beside one of Mr. Nixon's more imaginative assistants. He laughed when I said that I felt at the moment like beating hell out of the chanters. "They're just having fun," he said. "That's what it is for them—fun, a festival." It was a festival for Nixon, too. Two, maybe three, rocks had flown in his direction from a clutch of protesters at Burlington. He had mentioned rock-throwers at every subsequent stop and would continue to mention them the following week. He had his lines on obscene dissent down pat before he left Washington, he had been using them all day, and the final episode at the Green Bay airport said all there is to say about the uses to which he and his staff were putting the strident young. A police officer came up to two patrolmen standing beside one of the floodlight banks and said in my hearing: "The minute the President steps out on the ramp, turn the lights on this bunch," nodding toward the chanters. When the patrolmen indicated disbelief, the officer said, "That's what they want us to do —*now do it!*"

Mr. Nixon emerged, most of the people yelled their welcome, and the floodlights fixed the choralists in a white glare. After a terse salute to his candidates ("the next Governor . . . the next United States Senator . . . your own John Byrnes"), the President looked toward the protesters, who were still shouting, and said his piece. He seemed to know that it wasn't coming off as planned: the crowd was looking at him, not at his targets; he was too far away; it was too obviously staged, even for him, the only bobbled performance that I observed in three days of skilled performances at the start of an effort that would take him from coast to coast, to some 20 states. Visibly embarrassed and fumbling for the right words,

the President spoke his lines anyway: "Let me say that I respect
their right to be heard even if they do not respect my right to be
heard. And let me say also, ladies and gentlemen, I can assure
them that they are a very live minority in this country, but they are
a minority, and it is time for the majority to stand up and be
counted. The way you can be counted is not by trying to shout
speakers down, not by throwing rocks, not by bombing buildings,
not by shouting obscenities, but I will tell you how you can be
counted: with the most quiet, powerful voice in the world, by voting on November 3 for Jack Olson, John Erickson, and John
Byrnes." It got a satisfactory cheer, though not the thunderous response that the same call upon "the great silent majority" to set
itself apart from the young and violent and obscene minority elic-
ited in later appearances in Ohio and Nebraska, in Missouri and
Tennessee, North Carolina and Indiana. As he did everywhere else,
in rain and cold, sunshine and darkness, the President then went to
the crowd in Green Bay—not to the chanters but to his friends in
the darkness beyond the lights, reaching for their out-reached
hands, telling them they were wonderful people.

All of the states, Pennsylvania excepted, that the President chose
for his first forays gave him majorities in 1968 and had Senators,
mostly Democrats, who had opposed him on major issues. That
anomaly provided his central theme. It was "whether or not the
President . . . gets the power to do what he promised to do." He
was pleading for a strong and effective Presidency, presenting himself as a President who could be strong and effective only if he had
the support in Congress and particularly in the Senate that (as he
told it) the Democratic majorities in both houses had denied him.
The Republican indifference and opposition which had substantially
contributed to his troubles with two of the domestic measures that
he cited in every speech—revenue sharing and welfare reform—
were not mentioned. His surviving bitterness over the rejection of
his Southern nominees for the Supreme Court, Clement Haynes-
worth and Harrold Carswell, became ever more obvious at success-
sive stops, but there was no reminder that Republican votes against
both nominations made the deciding difference. Those and his
other searing difficulties—on war policy, on the ABM, on appropriations in excess of his budget requests—were blamed now only

on such Democrats as Quentin Burdick in North Dakota, Albert Gore in Tennessee, Stuart Symington in Missouri, Birch Bayh and Vance Hartke in Indiana. One wondered, watching such Republican dissidents as Clifford Case in New Jersey and William Saxbe in Ohio, posturing and smiling at the President's side in their states, how some of his simplifications really affected them. But that kind of thought seemed to be by the way, a nasty irrelevancy, during Mr. Nixon's preelection show of a master politician at work.

Mr. Nixon never during the first days on the road let up on his play of the "great silent majority" against the young and vocal minority, even when representatives of the latter failed to favor him with obtrusive manifestations. Always he managed to get back to that subject, and always in the terms that he used in Green Bay. At Columbus, Ohio, he was at his worst and his best in dealing with it. The usual chorus, mostly provided by students from Ohio State University, was in evidence when he addressed a big throng on the capitol grounds. Two girls with long blonde hair, in their mid and late teens, made their way into the privileged area just beneath the podium where the President spoke. Silent, edging steadily forward, looking up at him, they made the V sign for peace with their right hands. He saw them, looked away, looked down at them again, and swallowed—hard. Then, never pausing in his speech, he pulled his eyes away from them and did not look their way again. Afterward, he broke away from most of his press party and had himself driven, unannounced, to the Ohio State campus. It was a courageous thing to do and he did it well. A few four-letter chanters mobilized and were told to shut up by the hundreds of students who surrounded him. For 18 minutes the President talked to them of his will for peace, they talked to him of war, and they and he listened to each other. He used the episode later, with the inevitable exaggerations, in dubious proof that the dissenting minority was as small and vicious—he used that word—and as detested by the student majority as he said it was. Even so, the accounts of the few reporters who witnessed the exchange at Ohio State made me think better of Mr. Nixon than I did when I watched him in his brief and silent and craven exchange with the girls who made the V sign at him on the capitol steps.

October 31, 1970

XXXII

Welfare
and Muscle

A test of the President's good faith and of the Senate's intelligence and humanity is in the offing. It is coming when Congress reconvenes after the election recess and the Senate Finance Committee resumes its prolonged diddling with the measure that Mr. Nixon has called "the most important piece of domestic legislation proposed by this Administration." Whether he meant it when he spoke in that way of the welfare reforms embodied in his Family Assistance Act, and whether first the Finance Committee and then the Senate as a whole are capable of approving those reforms, even in embryo, will be demonstrated in the four to six weeks that remain of this congressional session.

Nothing infuriates Mr. Nixon's people more than the suggestion that his good faith in this matter needs to be demonstrated. "There is nothing," Counselor Daniel P. Moynihan said in August, "that so baffles the mind of a White House assistant as the question, 'Has the President supported this program?' " The question should not

baffle so bright a fellow as Pat Moynihan, who hopes against hope
that enough of the original program will survive the ministrations
of the Finance Committee and a doubtful future on the Senate floor
to be remembered as his monument, the great achievement of his
Nixon service, when he leaves the White House and returns to Harvard in early 1971. Mr. Nixon has in fact supported Family Assistance, but with nothing like the vigor that he applied in his fights for
the ABM, for his rejected Supreme Court nominations, and against
amendments that would have restricted his freedom to end or pro-
long the Vietnam war as he chooses. The President and his staff
intimates speak often in their private counsels of what they call his
"muscle," the actual influence and pressure that he can bring to
bear upon senators and representatives to get his way in a Congress
controlled by Democratic majorities. White House muscle is a ra-
tioned commodity, and the amount of it expended upon welfare
reform has been judiciously limited. Mr. Nixon prefers the soft sell
to the hard sell in his dealings with Congress, in any case, and his
personal "sell" for Family Assistance has been so soft that some of
the legislators who want to enact his program leave his presence
wondering whether he wants it as much as they do.

Chairman Russell Long and four other members of the Finance
Committee had a typical experience with the President on September 3. Mr. Nixon arranged for them to be flown from Washington
to the California White House in San Clemente, with their wives
and in a government plane, on their way to a dinner for the President of Mexico in San Diego. Moynihan and George Shultz, a senior White House assistant who as Secretary of Labor had shaped
up the Nixon program for congressional action, flew out with the
senators. They included the only two active friends of the bill on
the committee, Abraham Ribicoff of Connecticut, a Democrat, and
Wallace Bennett of Utah, the sole committee Republican supporting it. The others were Paul Fannin of Arizona and Jack Miller of
Iowa, two Republicans who were respectively against it and maybe
open to arguments for it. Their hour and more of private talk with
the President in San Clemente could have been crucial for the Administration's effort to break the bill, already passed by the House,
out of the committee and onto the Senate floor for a decisive vote.
Nixon assistants later said that the President "really laid it on the
line," telling the senators and particularly the Republicans in forth-
right fashion that he wanted it out and wanted it soon. That was

not the recollection of two of the senators. They said that they and their colleagues did most of the talking, that Mr. Nixon "just listened, mostly" and that all of them left the President with a feeling that, sure, he wanted the bill enacted, but not badly enough to make them sorry if it wasn't reported out and passed.

Mr. Nixon singled out his welfare program for frequent mention during his preelection campaigning in October. He did it in a curious fashion, perhaps tactically sound but hardly calculated to generate support for the positive reforms in his program. His campaign audiences would never have known from what he said about it that its great social virtue, the advance in welfare practice that could make it historic, lies in its promise of a guaranteed minimal income, underwritten by the federal government, for every American family. He did not even hint in his October speeches at the supplementary program of federally guaranteed medical insurance that he has promised to submit to Congress in early 1971. Instead he reverted to his 1968 campaign line, placing his major emphasis upon the requirement that adult recipients who can work or be trained for work will have to work or get off welfare. He spoke of the federal obligation "to provide adequately for the needs of all the people . . . a floor of dignity on which to stand." But his heavy thrust, the one that brought the cheers, came when he said, "Let's quit subsidizing those who are able to work, can have jobs or could get them and refuse to take them." The intended effect was what it had been in 1968, to equate welfare reform with getting the bums off welfare—although in fact, as demonstrated by the Administration's own data, the proportion of employable and deliberate loafers on welfare in all of its forms is so low as to be statistically negligible. The line taken by the President could have been, and some of his assistants said it was, a device to make his positive reforms more acceptable to conservative candidates for whom he was campaigning and to the conservative incumbents with whom he had to deal in the Senate. If so, he was paying a heavy price in terms of true public understanding of the measure on which the President has staked his principal claim to social enlightenment.

The congressional history of welfare reform put Mr. Nixon's campaign pitch that he needs Republican majorities in a ludicrous perspective. He owed House passage of Family Assistance largely to the Democratic chairman of the Ways and Means Committee, Wilbur Mills. In campaigning for the reelection of that committee's ranking Republican, John Byrnes of Wisconsin, the President never mentioned his support of welfare reform. The opposition of Senate Finance Committee Republicans, notably retiring John Williams of Delaware, had blocked the bill there since May. Bennett of Utah, the only Republican member on whom the President could count for support, had some serious reservations and was not at all certain that he would fight for the full Nixon program. Long of Louisiana, the Democratic chairman, kept assuring the President's lobbyists that he would send something to the floor and they literally grovelled before him to hold his negative and uncertain support. Ribicoff of Connecticut, who could qualify as one of Vice President Agnew's Democratic "radical liberals," had done more to save the bill from complete defeat than any other committeeman, in either party. HEW Secretary Elliot Richardson, who carried the main burden for the Administration in tireless lobbying for the bill, would have been lost without Ribicoff, and Family Assistance would have no chance at all if other committee Democrats did not come up with a support that they so far had withheld.

It was true, as Nixon assistants reminded the press, that such liberals as Gore of Tennessee, Hartke of Indiana (both caught in close races for reelection), Eugene McCarthy of Minnesota (retiring this year and preoccupied with other matters), and Harris of Oklahoma (for reform in principle, but also for higher benefits and wider coverage than the Administration wants) had been remarkably languid in their attitudes toward a program that should have won them from the start. The suspicion that some Senate Democrats just didn't want a Republican Administration credited with so promising a reform was not altogether groundless. But it was equally true that Senate Republicans had been for the most part either indifferent or obstructive.

The result is what might be expected. The most the Administration hopes to get out of the committee and past the Senate is a limited pilot program, to be tried out in three or four states and localities and to become effective nationally no earlier than July 1972. The prospect at best is a sad ending to a social effort that should have been the Administration's finest.

November 7, 1970

BULLHORN

XXXIII

Is Agnew Washed Up?

Nothing could improve my opinion of Richard Nixon more than believable evidence that Vice President Agnew's performance during the 1970 political campaign washed him up with the President and caused Mr. Nixon to begin looking around for another running mate in 1972. *Newsweek,* this journal's *TRB,* and David S. Broder, the chief political writer of *The Washington Post,* found it credible in the last days of the campaign that Mr. Nixon might be in the market for another Vice President. Broder reported in the *Post* of October 27, the day before Mr. Nixon spoke in Texas in behalf of Congressman George Bush's candidacy for the Senate, that "the firm conviction of men intimately involved in White House political operations" was that the President would dump Agnew and replace him with Bush if Bush won his Senate race—which he didn't.

The only aspect of this and similar speculation that is dealt with here is the notion, from which all of the speculation rises, that the Vice President's performance displeased and disappointed the Pres-

ident. If Mr. Nixon revises his estimate of Spiro T. Agnew between
now and 1972 and comes to prefer another candidate for the Vice
Presidency, as of course he may, it won't be because Agnew did
anything that he wasn't supposed to do or did it less well than the
President expected in 1970. Probably no political campaign, and
certainly none in which Mr. Nixon has been involved, has been
more carefully devised and supervised by an incumbent President
than this campaign was. One of its successes, election results apart,
was the extent to which the media, the public, and many politicians
were gulled into regarding Agnew with his silly alliterations, his
brutal and misleading attacks upon "radical liberals," his whole
strategy of divisive polarization, as a personality and a voice apart
and distinct from Richard Nixon. The Agnew who mounted the
stump at Springfield, Illinois, on September 10 and finished up at
Boise, Idaho, on October 31 spoke often of "my assignment" and
"my mission," meaning the assignment given him and the mission
defined for him by the President. He was Nixon's puppet, he knew
it, and—as he said in Boise—he found his campaign role "not only
exciting and a lot of fun, but also immensely fulfilling."

Mr. Nixon began shaping up the Agnew assignment in July and
August of 1969. It was decided then to put the Vice President on
the road and test his popular appeal with the series of attacks upon
the media, "impudent snobs," "rotten apples," and "so-called intellectuals" that made him an effective national personality—so effective, in fact, that some of the President's assistants then turned
their minds to the problem of how to use Agnew for the President's
purposes and still keep him under adequate control. There followed
some months of relative restraint, a narrowing of the Agnew targets
from the offended poor and black and young to such public figures
as senators who opposed Nixon actions and policies, foreign and
domestic. Agnew during this period functioned pretty much on his
own, though always (as he said) within understood limits of what
the President wanted and expected of him. That phase ended publicly and officially on August 6, when the Vice President was allowed to announce for himself that White House Counselor Bryce
N. Harlow and four other Nixon men had been assigned to assist
him during the mid-term campaign. They did more than assist.
They produced the Agnew performance, and they did it along lines
originally prescribed and rechecked throughout the operation by
Mr. Nixon himself. The chief producer was Harlow, acting for the

President in day-to-day concert with H. R. (Bob) Haldeman, Mr. Nixon's administrative chief of staff, who had much to do in his quiet way with devising the total campaign strategy and was charged with seeing that it was executed as the President wished.

A word about Bryce Harlow is in order before we return to the matter of whether Agnew finished himself with Nixon by serving Nixon. Harlow's association with the President dates back to the Eisenhower years, when he was a White House assistant and was often assigned to help the then Vice President. His loyalty to Mr. Nixon is total, his standing with the President is high. Perhaps more to the present point, Bryce Harlow is very good at evading difficult questions (such as whether he planned to leave the Nixon staff). But he is no good at lying to reporters, and during an acquaintance that began in the 1950s I have never caught him lying to me. When I asked him about the reports that Mr. Nixon was unhappy with Mr. Agnew and was minded to dump him, Harlow answered: "That is entirely, absolutely false. I have no idea where that stuff is coming from. I've seen some of the stories, and some of them cite a White House source. If there is one, it is somebody speaking subjectively and for himself and not for the White House or the President. You can just throw it out—it's entirely false."

In the course of the inquiries that led me to Harlow, I heard it said at the White House and at the Republican National Committee headquarters that none other than Deputy Counsel Murray M. Chotiner might be leaking the stories of disaffection with Agnew. That was a startler, for Chotiner is a tough political pragmatist and long-time Nixon associate who specializes in devising just the kind of ruthless tactics that Agnew personified and practiced during the campaign. It was Chotiner, not Agnew, who initiated and pursued to its disgraceful and intended conclusion the process of excommunicating Republican Senator Charles Goodell of New York and thereby demonstrating to other dissident Republican liberals the perils of opposing their Republican President. Without putting Chotiner in the Harlow class of habitual nonliars, I credit him with sense enough not to tell lies that he could be caught at. When he was asked what he thought of Agnew's campaign effort, he said: "I think that it's been of great assistance to the candidates whom he has been supporting and that all this talk is coming from the opposition to the Vice President." As to the stories: "I haven't the slightest idea where they are coming from." When told that some people who function in his vicinity thought they might be coming from him, Chotiner said: "That not only is a figment of the imagination, but somebody must have had a nightmare. There is not one word of truth to it—directly, indirectly, or remotely."

Two of the President's staff Counselors, Robert H. Finch and Daniel P. Moynihan, have made their distaste for Agnewism well known in Washington. Moynihan is not consulted on political matters. Finch is, though not to the extent that reporters were led to think he would be early in the 1970 campaign. Instead of managing the campaign for the President from the White House, as he was expected to do, Finch spent most of his time and energies on the road in September and October, speaking for Nixon policies and Nixon Republicans in 25 states. His pitch differed in a significant way from that of the President and the Vice President. "If we can build a record of effectiveness, compassion and concern across all the boundaries of race and age and religion," Finch said in his standard speech, "then we will indeed build a new Republican majority over the face of this nation." Given such a record, he went about the country saying, "we will become the majority party—*and we will deserve to be.*" Compassion and concern in the Finch meaning of the words, and the implicit suggestion that the Republican Party with another kind of record might not deserve to be "the majority party," were strikingly absent from both Nixon's and Agnew's speeches. It would be nice to think that the Finch view may prevail with Mr. Nixon, now that the election is past. But the modest role assigned to Finch and the fact that the White House publicity apparatus ignored his speeches do not suggest that it will.

There's been talk that Finch, a former lieutenant governor of California with sound claims to political effectiveness when he is given his head, may be shifted from the White House staff to the chairmanship of the Republican National Committee in the place of Congressman Rogers C. B. Morton of Maryland. If that happens, it won't necessarily signify a meaningful ideological change. Morton is also a moderate, he would like to have a Cabinet job (maybe the one held by Secretary of the Interior Walter Hickel), and the working relationship between his committee organization and the President's staff politicians has been anything but happy. Morton's deputy chairman, James Allison, a former Texas newspaper publisher and professional campaign operative, is of a mind to leave the committee for one of the reasons that make Morton less than anxious to stay on. The reason is that the President and his staff people, Bob Haldeman in particular, have insisted upon running the GOP's national political operation from the White House. Directives signed by Haldeman have not encouraged Morton and Allison to believe that they are the responsible party builders that they are supposed to be.

A bit of by-play in connection with the possible replacement of Morton by Finch illuminates the kind of thinking that goes into Nixon political management. It so happens that Finch, when he was Secretary of Health, Education, and Welfare, gained an undeserved reputation in the South for hard-nosed enforcement of school desegregation. Harry Dent of South Carolina, the President's staff Southerner, was sitting around with some of the boys one evening, discussing the talk of Finch-for-Morton. The others assumed that Dent would oppose such an appointment, on the ground that it would offend Southern Republicans and impede the effort to develop a successful Southern Republican party. Finch in the national chairmanship certainly wouldn't help, Dent said, but there might be a way around that difficulty if the President wanted to make the change. The Southerners could be told that it might be better for them to have Finch at the national committee, in a spot that had been proved to be largely honorific, than in his present place at the center of real power in the White House.

Now that the elections are over, with their limited and mixed rewards for the immense effort put into the 1970 campaign by the President and his Vice President, it may be assumed that a lot of thinking and rethinking will be going on at the Nixon power center. The controlling calculation that Middle America is conservative country and that Vice President Agnew speaks effectively for and appeals effectively to it should be in for reexamination. Agnew did exactly what he was instructed to do, exactly in the way he was told to do it, and the President capped the Agnew performance with his own, on exactly the same lines, and it didn't work as well as it was expected to work.

The question is, how will Mr. Nixon evaluate these facts? What, if anything, will he learn from them? My guess is that he will learn very little. Mr. Nixon's performance in the campaign tells an interesting thing about him. He campaigned in 1970 precisely as he did in 1968, with the same mannerisms, the same catchlines, the same display of a gut instinct that repels at least as many people as it

attracts. In this respect, nearly two years in the Presidency taught
him nothing and changed nothing.

November 14, 1970

For the fates of Hickel and Morton, see Chapters 35 and 36.

XXXIV

Love That Pap

Mr. Nixon's reported opinion that the mid-term election results amounted to an enormous ideological success for him and the Republican Party and practically assured his reelection in 1972 was dominating the news, and was being ridiculed by many pundits, when I decided that it was up to me to save the President from his folly. Surely, I told various underlings to tell their bosses at the White House and the federal departments, the pap that was being attributed to him and fed to the press by some of his assistants and political advisers did not represent Mr. Nixon's actual view of the results. Surely this President—this "master politician"—could not really believe that a net loss of eleven Republican governorships and nine Republican seats in the House of Representatives, and a net gain of two or at most three Senate seats in a year when 25 Democratic seats were contested, added up to the victory that he himself had rather hesitantly claimed in California on the day after the election and was said to be claiming, in the most glowing and positive terms, in later sessions with his Cabinet, with his White House assistants, and with selected columnists. If I was right in assuming (I said) that this was in large part contrived nonsense,

"THE ELECTION WAS A VICTORY, BUT WE'LL TRY TO STAY HUMBLE ABOUT IT."

understandably intended to counter the general impression that the President and his party had emerged from the election with, at best, a result somewhere between a standoff and a defeat, I'd be glad to report as much and so do my bit toward restoring Richard Nixon's political credibility.

The consequences were educational. Only Attorney General John N. Mitchell, among the Nixon advisers and assistants who were thus approached, refused to discuss the matter. He sent word that he wasn't about to talk politics and discuss the election results with any reporter just then. The others, Cabinet members and White House assistants alike, said as in one voice that the only pap involved was my supposition that Mr. Nixon did not really believe what he said he believed and was said by others to believe. He really had told his Cabinet and staff, as *Time* reported, that "the election, ideologically, was enormously successful" and that "you can give your friends in the press odds on the Presidential success in 1972." He actually was saying in private, and convincing those to whom he said it that he really believed it, that the election outcome guaranteed him "a working majority of four" and "an ideological majority of six" in the Senate on the defense and foreign policy issues that he considered critical.

Some of his most intimate associates and advisers said they believed that he believed, as he said publicly in California and continued to say privately in Washington and Florida, that "the majority has spoken, the real majority in this country" in support of him and of his major policies, foreign and domestic. The same associates said they had yet to hear the President utter one word of regret or give the slightest indication of second thoughts about his own performance in the final three weeks of the campaign—a performance that, in its carefully designed conjunction with that of Vice President Agnew, had seemed to me and others to demean him and the Presidency and to diminish both his capacity for national leadership and his chances of reelection in 1972.

The history of a postelection document distributed to the press and to many politicians by Counselor Robert H. Finch did more than anything that Finch and other Nixon associates said to convince me that the Nixon pap is not, in the President's actual view, pap at all but gospel truth. The document consisted of a letter signed by Finch and his "expanded notes" from what he had heard

the President say to the Cabinet, to the White House staff, and to a
group of nine columnists. Finch stated in the letter his "inescapable
conclusion" that "the President's campaign activity was clearly
among the decisive factors" and that "at the national level the Administration was clearly endorsed and the campaign a clear success." The notes, which were intended to be read as a summary of
the President's views and language, set forth in detail the argument
that the election results gave Mr. Nixon his "working majority" in
the Senate and presaged victory in 1972 on the strength of peace
abroad, order and prosperity at home. Finch suggested to the President, and Mr. Nixon authorized, the preparation and distribution
of the letter and notes. Finch took rough drafts with him to Florida, where he and other assistants conferred with the President on
November 7, and left copies for review by the President and by
H. R. Haldeman, the Nixon chief of staff. Haldeman telephoned Mr.
Nixon's final okay to Finch in Washington and suggested a few
changes. Herbert Klein, the President's Director of Communications, sent out the approved version on White House stationery,
completing a sequence which should remove any doubt that Mr.
Nixon not only wants it known and believed that he perceives a
genuine victory in the results but takes a major share of credit for
it.

The claim of immediate victory, 1972 prospects aside, rests
mainly upon Mr. Nixon's reading of the Senate results. His reading
differs drastically from that of several incumbent Republican senators. Robert Packwood of Oregon, who rates himself a Nixon loyalist, compared the Republican opportunities with the results and
found the outcome "a disaster." Mark Hatfield of Oregon, hardly a
loyalist in the Packwood sense but still a sound Republican, said in
postelection speeches that Nixon and Agnew had wrongly divided
the country with their campaign rhetoric and tactics and were head-
ing the party toward defeat in 1972. Packwood and Hatfield were
among 19 Republican senators who denounced the Nixon-Agnew
rejection of Republican Senator Charles Goodell in New York and
did what they could, in protest, to avert his defeat by Conservative
James Buckley, one of Mr. Nixon's assumed "ideological majority."
A key figure in that same supposed majority, Democrat Lloyd
Bentsen of Texas, rushed up to Washington to declare in a press
conference and (he said) to tell Mr. Nixon in private that he pro-

posed to function in the Senate as a member of "the loyal opposition," with no blank checks promised or given to the President. Lowell Weicker of Connecticut, one of the Republican victors on whom the President counts, voted as a Representative against the President on two of three significant defense and foreign policy issues in the 1970 session and scored nine out of twelve on the liberal side in *The New Republic*'s rating of the 91st Congress. The facts are that the Senate Republicans are still a minority, that some of them are as ready now as they have been in the past to oppose the President on critical issues, and that the claim of a "working" and "ideological" majority in a Senate controlled by partisan Democrats is wishful balderdash.

The Nixon view of the election results is related to what the President thinks has been happening to the country since he took office. He genuinely believes, his associates say, that his "real majority . . . the great silent majority" has taken effective charge and that he has established himself with that supposed majority as its surrogate. His attitude of cold disdain toward antiwar protesters in 1969, tempered by a limited show of toleration early in 1970, is thought at the White House to have accomplished a major victory for orderly policy processes over those who hoped to prevail by disorder. The simultaneous effort, personified and led by Vice President Agnew, to identify the President's liberal critics and opponents, in both parties, with the disorderly and, to Mr. Nixon's majority, the most repellent elements in American society, is believed by men who presumably reflect his beliefs to have succeeded to a degree and in ways that are imperfectly reflected in the election results but nevertheless justify his optimistic view of the basic trends. A further assumption at the White House is that all of this is quite obvious to the legislators, Republican and Democratic, and particularly to the senators with whom the President will be dealing in the next Congress. The President's purpose in the recent campaign, the purpose to which he specifically assigned Spiro Agnew, was to promote the identification of himself and of his policies with the public yearning for peace-and-order and to carry forward the process, already well begun, of identifying his opposition—the Vice President's "radical liberals"—with disorder. If the President believes, as he is said to believe, that he has in fact assured himself of an "ideological majority" in the Senate and, by implication, in the country at large, he has to believe that this cynical and ruthless campaign of "constructive polarization" (Agnew's phrase) succeeded in 1970 and will succeed again in 1972.

November 28, 1970

XXXV

Hickel's Hot Seat

"Of course there will be changes as we go along," Mr. Nixon's press spokesman said the other day, coming as close as the President would then allow to confirming a spate of rumors that he intends to enter the second half or his first term with a substantially altered Cabinet and White House team, "I will have no comment on all of this speculation," the spokesman said a little later, "until we have something to announce, if and when we have anything to announce."

One of the changes yet to be announced was the nomination of Counselor Daniel P. Moynihan, the President's senior staff Democrat and somewhat tarnished expert on problems ranging from urban reform to narcotics control, to be the US Ambassador to the United Nations. It was a strange reassignment, so strange for so many reasons that it indicated a yen for change for change's sake on the President's part that brought his own powers of judgment into question. Without officially confirming the President's intention, those mysterious characters known to the press as "White House sources" dished up several justifications, including Pat Moynihan's flair for graceful and spectacular public performances and his work over the past 18 months in trying to coordinate US and

NATO social policies. None of the justifications made much sense from either his or the President's standpoint. Mr. Nixon has made it plain that he does not regard the UN as a forum for the conduct of vital international business, apart from a few matters such as the admission of Communist China. The post has been an unsplendid misery for past ambassadors, Adlai Stevenson and Arthur Goldberg among them, who were inveigled into it for showcase purposes. The incumbent, career diplomat Charles W. Yost, has proved himself to be suited by training and temperament for a job that by a historic definition requires strict adherence to instructions laid down by the State Department and White House and promises nothing but grief for ambassadors who try to operate in the freewheeling Moynihan style. For reasons that in my opinion are unfair to him, Moynihan is held in very low regard by black Americans and he may expect a cold welcome from the UN's black Africans.

Other prospective changes loomed larger in the news and stayed in the news because the President wanted them there. Undoubtedly at his behest, his assistants played the printed and other media like an organ, feeding out and then coyly discouraging rumors that Secretaries David Kennedy of the Treasury, Maurice Stans of Commerce, George Romney of Housing and Urban Development, Clifford Hardin of Agriculture, and Walter Hickel of Interior were candidates for early replacement. Hardin only excepted ("absolutely without foundation," a Nixon spokesman said of that rumor after it had emerged from the White House), the victims were deliberately allowed to squirm in the resultant uncertainty. It was Mr. Nixon's way, as it had been the way of past Presidents, of softening the ground for any changes that he may finally decide upon. Attorney General John N. Mitchell, also a subject of rumor, acted as the President's preliminary executioner in at least two instances. George Romney acknowledged, obliquely and in obvious pain, that Mitchell had forewarned him of a possible change. Walter Hickel confided to his favorite TV interviewer, Mike Wallace of CBS, that Mitchell had advised him to "sit tight until you hear from me again. So, I'm sitting tight."

Secretary Hickel has been sitting tight in a heated seat for longer than is generally known. His dismal beginning at a pre-inaugural press conference, when his crude indications that he had no use for "conservation for conservation's sake" outraged many people, and his rapid recovery with a series of highly publicized and surpris-

ingly bold actions in behalf of conservation, have long since become parts of the Hickel legend. So has a letter that he addressed
to the President in May of 1970, suggesting that Vice President
Agnew be muzzled and that Mr. Nixon pay hitherto unaccustomed
heed both to dissident youth and to his own Cabinet members. The
recurrent rumors since then that Mr. Nixon could do without Secretary Hickel have been taken as evidence that the President never
forgave Hickel, not so much for the letter as for the fact that Hickel
leaked the letter to three newspapers before it arrived at the White
House. Well before that, however, Hickel was in disfavor with some
of the President's assistants if not with Mr. Nixon.

John D. Ehrlichman, a Nixon assistant who still has more dealings with Hickel than any other staff man and is regarded in Hickel
quarters as one of the Secretary's few White House friends, began
to hear early in the Administration that the Interior Department,
never a model of administrative efficiency, was going pretty much
to pot. Hickel's relationship with Under Secretary Russell Train, a
dedicated conservationist who had been installed principally to off-
set the Secretary's poor reputation in that field, was known to be
practically nonexistent. Hickel, a land developer and builder who
was governor of Alaska when Nixon brought him to Washington,
was reported at the White House to communicate only with a
coterie of immediate assistants, several of them imported with him
from Alaska, and to be playing a lone and egoistic role that was
having disastrous effects upon the department's management. Ehrlichman assigned a staff to check these reports, found them largely
true, and confronted Hickel with them. Hickel admitted that the
criticism had merit and promised to correct the causes. Russell
Train, now chairman of the statutory Council on Environmental
Quality, was succeeded by an Under Secretary who was thought to
be a whiz at management and has not been heard from since. The
judgment at the White House, even among officials who admire
Hickel's record in conservation and his efforts to bring the Administration into tune with dissatisfied young Americans, is that Interior's management continues to be distressingly poor.

The difficulty between the two men may be more a matter of
temperament than anything else. Nixon, with his passion for orderly
and quiet operation except when he himself chooses to get raucous,
is not likely to be or remain enamoured of a Secretary who fights
back at his secret detractors with remarks like "The President hired

me and he will have to fire me" and who delights in proclaiming
that Mr. Nixon will have to offer a mighty good reason if and when
he demands the resignation of Walter J. Hickel. If and when the
President demands it, he will be depriving himself of a Secretary
who has earned the plaudits of such congressional conservationists
as Sen. Mark Hatfield of Oregon and of Rep. Henry S. Reuss of
Wisconsin, the Democratic chairman of an important conservation
subcommittee. "Secretary Hickel has been a pleasant surprise,"
Reuss says. "My net judgment is that on a wide variety of issues he
has been right." One of the several issues on which Hickel has been
right, in the judgment of Reuss and others of like mind, is the control of industrial dumping of mercury. Reuss blames Attorney
General Mitchell, not Hickel, for a failure to enforce tough Interior
Department regulations with court action. Hickel's record in this
matter, Reuss says, "is as good as Mitchell's is bad. Mitchell's is
horrible."

Secretary Hickel's duration in office may turn upon the biggest
and toughest of all the ecological issues that he has dealt with. This
is the proposal to drive an oil line through 800 miles of virgin
Alaska, from recently discovered fields on the North Slope to a
warm-water port. The pressures upon Hickel from his home state
to grant the necessary permits, regardless of the demonstrably disastrous ecological effects, have been enormous and he has resisted
them more effectively than a Secretary with his background could
have been expected to do. The stringent stipulations that he has
imposed may be held to constitute, with their ghastly citations of
the minimum harm that is certain to be done, a convincing argument that the pipeline should not be allowed under any conditions.

Short of that Draconian choice, Secretary Hickel has refused to
grant the permits until and unless his protective requirements are
met. Months of struggle with the opposed interests lie ahead, but
Walter Hickel will not be around at Interior to settle that problem,
or any other.

December 5, 1970

———

This report went to press in *The New Republic* two hours before the President fired Walter Hickel and two days before the White House announced that Pat Moynihan would not be the next Ambassador to the United Nations.

XXXVI

At Battle Stations

You are talking with a friend in a West Wing office at the White House, at the quiet end of a day that has been a frantic one for him, when he drops a remark that answers most of your questions. The questions have to do with a sensed change in the climate around Mr. Nixon, a hardening of the Presidential attitudes that pervade the place and condition the attitudes and labors of all who serve the President. Are the change and the hardening real? They are, the friend says, and they are natural and inevitable if one considers a determining difference between the first two years and the second two years of this Nixon term. "We are taking battle stations for 1972," the President's man says. Mr. Nixon wants and expects to be reelected then, his thoughts and plans and policies are centered upon that objective, and everything that he does and causes to happen at the White House and throughout government must in the nature of things be related to it.

There is, for example, the matter of Counselor Daniel P. Moynihan and the evidence that the President neither wishes nor intends to replace him when he returns to the Harvard faculty in early 1971. Happily for him, though he refused to recognize the reasons why it was a happy decision, Moynihan changed his mind about accepting the President's offer of the US ambassadorship to the United Nations but stuck to his belief that two years on the Nixon staff were enough. It turns out that Moynihan and the President between them had cooked up, in seven months of lively discussion, an odd and intriguing but impossible notion of what the UN ambassadorship could be made into. Excepting only the stormy tenure of Henry Cabot Lodge in the Eisenhower years, the ambassadorship has been a glorified messenger's job, intensely frustrating for incumbents who tried to make it anything more than the obedient calling of Washington's signals. Moynihan and Nixon talked themselves into believing that the UN could be regarded as a sort of international welfare state, rarely adapted to serious and conventional diplomatic business but ideally suited to the display of Moynihan's dual expertise in social problems and international relations (which he studied before he became an urban specialist). Premature disclosure embarrassed the President and raised some personal difficulties for Moynihan. He and Nixon sadly agreed on the morning of November 25 to call off a plan that, if it had been carried out, would almost certainly have proved to be mistaken and impractical.

The remaining point of interest is the President's indicated conclusion that he won't need Pat Moynihan or his equivalent at the White House in the second two years of his term. The reason stated there is that it was safe and feasible in the first two years to encourage a certain amount of innovative thinking and programming of the kind in which Moynihan and the young men whom he brought to the White House with him specialized. Most of the proposals that they stimulated and developed—for welfare reform, higher education, mass transport, the beginnings of a national health care system, among others—were dead or languishing in Congress toward the end of 1970. Less energy went into getting them enacted than into getting them proposed. But they added up to a more extensive and more impressive body of potential legislation than was generally expected of the Nixon Administration. And now Pat Moynihan is leaving and the last of his young men are leaving with or soon after him, not in most instances because of specific ideological differences with the President, but because they have sensed that the time for innovation is past. They perceive that the second two years is to be a time for caution, for disciplined adherence to declared Nixon doctrine, and above all for sustained appeal and submission to the conservative preferences and prejudices of the President's "great silent majority."

It took President Nixon just 25 minutes at the close of the day before Thanksgiving to fire his Cabinet maverick, Secretary of the Interior Walter Hickel, and to designate for his successor Congressman Rogers C. B. Morton of Maryland, the chairman of the Republican National Committee, who may be counted upon (as Hickel surprisingly could not be) to combine moderately enlightened ecological policies with a judicious respect for political necessities. The central actor in a drama that followed at the Interior Department may be regarded as a prototype of the ascendant Nixon man. He is Frederick V. Malek, aged 33, a California management consultant who made himself a fast fortune by putting together a conglomerate of tool companies and was placed at the Department of Health, Education, and Welfare to handle personnel problems for Secretary Robert H. Finch. Soon after Finch was transferred to the White House staff, Malek turned up there as a special assistant responsible for "recruiting top candidates to Presidential and other high-level appointive positions." He is personable, soft of voice and gentle in manner, and utterly cold in his approach to his job.

Malek went to the Interior Department and in one afternoon summarily fired six of its officials. Some of them had been so closely identified with Hickel that no successor would want them around. That was not true of Leslie Glasgow, the assistant secretary for wildlife, fish, and national parks. In Congress and elsewhere, among conservationists and others familiar with his work and concerns, he was known as a knowledgeable and effective ecologist who refused to truckle to despoilers, argued strongly for his own views of what policy should be, and loyally supported contrary policies when he was overruled. When Glasgow objected that he had been appointed by the President and should be fired by the President if by anyone, Malek said that he was speaking for the President and demanded an oral resignation then and there. A White House official involved in the unpleasant business said later that the firings were not quite as brutal as news accounts indicated:

the fired officials had been told, for instance, that they would be
paid for another month and could take their time about vacating
their offices. But, the official said, only Press Secretary Ronald
Ziegler could say as much for the record. Ziegler declined to say it
and so to soften the impression of savage reprisal that then prevailed. Could it be, the more informative official was asked, that
the President's people wanted an impression of ruthless White
House discipline to prevail throughout the federal bureaucracy?
"Maybe they do," the official answered.

One of Malek's assignments in early December was to find a
successor to Dr. Roger Egeberg, HEW's assistant secretary for
health services. Between denials at HEW and refusals to deny at
the White House that Egeberg was on the block, the report to that
effect was left in the weird realm of encouraged speculation that the
President evidently thought conducive to his preparations for the
preelection period. An enormous flap over possible appointees preceded Dr. Egeberg's selection for the job in 1969 and his acceptance of it was announced with maximum fanfare. The only explanation offered in private for the desire to get him out was that he
just didn't comprehend the ways and processes of government,
however good he might be at diagnosing the nation's health problems. It was a thin explanation, hesitantly advanced, and the same
kind of thing was said in the same way about Leslie Glasgow. It
hardly disposed of the supposition that both Egeberg and Glasgow
were judged to be unhappy with Nixon policy as they knew it.
That's the sort of thing that, in the second two Nixon years, won't
do at all.

December 12, 1970

———

Mr. Nixon came up in 1971 with some innovating proposals for
restructuring the federal government and sharing its revenue with
state and local governments. It will be seen in due course, I believe,
that they are fundamentally conservative proposals, much less
"revolutionary" in the true meaning of that term than the President
proclaimed them to be.

XXXVII

Blood
on the Floor

All of a sudden in early December Mr. Nixon succumbed to a desire to have it believed that he was as zealous in support of his welfare bill as were the few senators, mostly liberal Democrats, who were trying to improve and save it. He told James Farmer, who had grown tired of being the Nixon Administration's most prominent black official and had called at the White House to quit his job as an assistant secretary of Health, Education, and Welfare, to tell the press that the President had told him that "there will be blood on the floor" if Congress didn't pass an acceptable welfare bill. The President's staff lobbyists were telling him that what was left of his Family Assistance Plan had no better than a 50–50 chance of enactment in the last days of the 1970 session. If something reasonably like it was not enacted before adjournment, Nixon told Farmer to say for him, he would submit a revised version to the 92nd Congress and would personally lead the fight for it in 1971. His tepid leadership of the fight for the 1970 version accounted partly for the trouble it was in, and his talk about "blood on the floor" must have fascinated Republican senators who had been unaware of compelling Presidential pressure to support it.

The original Nixon proposal was pretty much intact when the House of Representatives approved and sent it along to the Senate Finance Committee in May 1970. The central features, the ones that justified the claim that it constituted a true advance in welfare practice, were a federal guarantee of a minimum income to dependent families with children, extension of supplemental federal assistance to families headed by "working poor" adults, and a start toward the substitution of uniform federal standards for the wide and discriminatory variations in state standards of need and support. The guaranteed minimum—$1000 a year for an adult and one child, $1600 for the commonly and somewhat deceptively cited "family of four"—was vulnerable low. But it was more than the poorest of the poor had to live on in much of the South and Appalachia. It could be and in most instances would be supplemented by a portion of earned wages and other income and by state payments. The Administration argued that most of the prospective 16 to 22 million benefited individuals, including dependents of "the working poor," would be enabled to live at levels considerably above the basic minima. However insufficient the minimum and actual income levels were, the recognition of a federal obligation to guarantee subsistence at some level was held to outweigh in importance the many objections that legitimately could be and were raised to the Nixon proposal. As the President made a great point of saying when he announced his program, it did not promise a "guaranteed income" to all needy Americans. But the principle of such a guarantee was implicit in it and the Nixon reform would have fared better than it did in the Senate committee if the President and his spokesmen had been courageous and honest enough to say so, instead of exaggerating the proportion of bums and loafers on welfare and promoting Family Assistance as a device to make them work and support themselves.

The opposition in the Finance Committee provided the best of all testimony that there was a lot of good in the program, despite the lengths to which the Administration went to minimize the good features and emphasize the bad ones in the misguided belief that liberal support could be taken for granted and that conservative support had to be won at any cost. The genuine reforms were simply too much for Russell Long of Louisiana, the chairman, and for five of the six Republicans on the committee. The same reforms were not enough for the liberal Democrats, among them Fred Harris of Oklahoma, Eugene McCarthy of Minnesota, Albert Gore of Tennessee, Vance Hartke of Indiana, and Abe Ribicoff of Connecticut. Both elements, the conservatives and the initially passive liberals, figured in the hassles that stalled the program from May into December and finally moved the President to threaten "blood on the floor."

First to satisfy the committee conservatives, and then to meet some of the objections of both conservatives and liberals, the Administration revised its proposals in June and again in October, and once again in late November. The basic provisions of the original program and of the House version survived these maneuvers and, toward the end of the 1970 struggle, the legislation remaining to be accepted or rejected by the Senate—if it had or took the time to do anything at all about it—was stronger than it had been at the low point of the committee phase. The problem of legislative time apart, the outcome and the future of welfare reform turned upon a few substantive issues.

The basic level of guaranteed support was not one of them, although it appeared to be. HEW Secretary Elliot Richardson agreed to accept, though not to recommend in a positive way, an increase in the symbolic family-of-four level from $1600 to $2200 by averaging out and paying in cash the value of food stamps that dependent families might otherwise receive, and to write into the legislation a higher goal to be aimed for at some unstated date. Even the aggressive and growing National Welfare Rights Organization, the only effective voice of welfare recipients, was prepared to settle for the goal instead of for the immediate $5500 it formally demanded, provided that the enacted legislation bound the federal government to meet the goal in a specified time. Other issues, going in essence to the relationship between citizens and their government, were actually more critical.

One of these issues was the requirement that employable or trainable family heads register for "suitable" jobs or training and forfeit their (but not their children's) share of federal support if they refused to accept the training or jobs to which they were assigned. The only substantial exceptions to this requirement were the mothers of children less than six years old. Since a high proportion of wholly dependent families are headed by mothers, many of them black, the federal pledge to provide adequate day care for the affected children did very little to soften a requirement that was at once cruel and unlikely to diminish the welfare rolls nearly as much as its defenders assumed. Senator Ribicoff asked, and Secretary Richardson went some way toward agreeing, that this "workfare" for mothers of school age children be modified. Senators Harris and McCarthy, encouraged by NWRO's insistent demand that no mother of school-age children be required to leave her home, called for its abolition.

The Administration proposed that employable adults be required to take any available and "suitable" job at "the prevailing wage." Senators Ribicoff, Harris, and McCarthy among others, emphatically supported by NWRO, argued that welfare adults should be required to take jobs only if they paid the federal minimum wage of $1.60 or the locally prevailing wage, whichever was higher. This issue was the subject of an interesting exchange between Harris and White House Counselor Daniel P. Moynihan, who had been billed (with some exaggeration) as the philosophical daddy of the Nixon program. Harris remarked to Moynihan that the question whether the national government should force any citizen to work for less than its own minimum wage went beyond economics and budgets, to the fundamentals of human rights. Moynihan exclaimed that he had never thought of it that way and, turning to HEW Under Secretary John Veneman, said, "Can't we do something about that, Jack?" The most the Administration could do about it, Secretary Richardson announced, was to accept a proviso that no recipient be made to work for less than $1.20 an hour, or three-fourths of the federal minimum. To require that welfare clients be paid at least the $1.60 minimum would be unfair, the Secretary said, to the seven million Americans not on welfare who work for less than that. Senator Harris and his allies prepared to fight on the floor, at some future date, for federal adherence to the federal minimum.

The budgetary bind that determined and limited many of the Administration positions on essentially human issues led Secretary Richardson to reject outright Senator Ribicoff's suggestion and Senator Harris's stronger insistence that the guaranteed federal payment rise with increases in cost-of-living indices. Throughout the welfare debate, the Administration had clung with desperate urgency to its stipulation that Family Assistance add no more than $4-billion-plus to the annual federal costs of public welfare. A mandatory cost-of-living trigger might initially add "as much as $400 million" to the anticipated expense, Secretary Richardson said, and that was more than the Administration would undertake.

The proposed approach to the imposition of uniform federal standards raised complex issues that were typical of the difficulties involved in any attempt to change a system as varied in its practices as state-administered welfare was bound to be. One such issue had to do with the special benefits—winter clothing for welfare children, furniture for underfurnished homes, emergency medical costs—that some states provide and some don't. NWRO and its senatorial friends, Harris and McCarthy among them, wanted to make certain that the effect of federalized welfare would not be to deprive present beneficiaries of any of these aids or of any part of the real income that they represented. The Administration argued with some reason that the principle of federally administered federal standards would in the end prove more important and beneficial than any forms of aid that might be temporarily lost, and that in any case the critics were assuming for tactical purposes that the worst that could happen was sure to happen. NWRO's formidable corps of lobbyists, mostly black and eloquent and amply proportioned ladies with children of their own and the strengths of actual experience with public welfare, and their executive director, a sometime professor of organic chemistry named George Wiley, asserted that the worst *was* certain to happen unless any new law specifically said that it was not to happen and the federal administrators were required to see that it didn't happen.

These arguments and many others complicated the situation that confronted Mr. Nixon and Congress at the close of what the President had intended to be his year for his version of welfare reform. His program, tattered at the edges but more nearly intact than it had seemed likely to be after six months of the Senate committee's capricious treatment of it, was neither the "gigantic fraud" that its extreme critics called it nor the sufficient reform that the President made it out to be in his equivocal and often misleading fashion. It was worth fighting for and saving, with all of its deficiencies, and the senators fighting for it most effectively in December were such committee liberals as Harris and Ribicoff. The sole

Republican on the Finance Committee who was of any real help continued to be Wallace Bennett of Utah. The committee record since May should have taught Mr. Nixon, but probably hadn't, that he would do well to turn from his conservative friends to the moderates and liberals in his own party and among the Democrats, if he were called upon in 1971 to exercise the personal leadership that he promised late in the welfare game.

December 19, 1970

The 91st Congress adjourned without enacting the welfare bill or even, in the Senate, bringing it to a vote. The President then gave it a high priority in his 1971 legislative program and began to emphasize its positive features of income support.

XXXVIII

This Is Conciliation?

Mr. Nixon's choices of a new Ambassador to the United Nations and a new Secretary of the Treasury may or may not turn out to be the triumphs of statesmanship and acumen that he obviously thought they were. But he unquestionably scored a triumph of another and, to him, perhaps more important kind. Judging by the general reporting of his activities in mid-December, he succeeded in purveying a notion that he had put his abrasive performance in the 1970 political campaign behind him. Now we had a different Nixon if not another "new Nixon." This different Nixon was in a mood to forgive his lately abused enemies and conciliate his critics. His problems in the next two years, the two years before the 1972 elections, were to be everybody's problems and particularly the Democrats' problems, and he was prepared and anxious to work them out in that generous spirit.

Such was the thrust, the attained objective, of the first press conference he had held in four months, and of the busy round of personal appearances that followed it. His success in projecting the desired impression was remarkable, considering the total content and meaning of what he said and did. Mr. Nixon did not give an inch of any issue that really mattered to him. His actual stance was tougher, his determination to get the things he wanted done in the way he wanted them done was firmer and more apparent than they had been before he set out to create an impression of conciliatory change.

He remarked at his press conference that he had expected more questions than he got about the 1970 elections and the outcome that he had previously called an enormous ideological success for his Administration and the Republican Party. The impression was left that he would have moderated that boast if he had been invited to. Maybe; but in fact he could have and didn't. He had campaigned "to the best of my ability" for candidates who would support him and afterward "I commented upon the election and gave my views on it." His responsibility "now that the people have spoken" was to work with the victors and he hoped that "Democrats and Republicans will work with the President." Would he again discard such Republican mavericks as Senator Charles Goodell of New York, who was branded a renegade at the President's instance and defeated? "Under no circumstances," Mr. Nixon said, affirming a pledge that he had already made in private to two worried Republican moderates, Senators Edward Brooke of Massachusetts and Charles Percy of Illinois. In 1972, he would support "all of those Republicans" who ran for the Senate. Some of them were "members of what is called the liberal wing of the party. But they are Republicans. We welcome them. We want them. We need both"—meaning, conservatives and liberals alike. It was said in the tone of a President who had made his point to the tolerated liberals and was content with the result.

A questioner suggested that he had, as his Scranton Commission on Campus Unrest had charged in a report neglected for 11 weeks, failed to convey to the country "a sufficiently sharp and clear sense of direction, vision and leadership." In his answers, orally at the conference and in a formal reply to the commission, Mr. Nixon acknowledged no failure whatever in that respect. Leadership was a task for many people other than the President, college administrators included, and he ranked one of the commission's particular though unnamed targets, Vice President Agnew, high among those who had given the country the kind of leadership it needed. The commission chairman, former Governor William Scranton of Pennsylvania, humbly thanked the President for at last commenting upon the report and saying that he had actually read it.

A question that went to the core of the President's domestic attitudes and policies was how far he proposed to go in using his wide federal powers "to promote racial integration in suburban housing." The President answered, "Only to the extent that the law requires," and he added for good measure: "I believe that forced integration of the suburbs is not in the national interest." It was the doctrine that had governed Mr. Nixon's approach to public school desegregation and that underlay his concept of national leadership—a concept that had been greatly narrowed since he said in 1968 that the next President's duty to America would be to "calm its angers, ease its terrible frictions, and bring its people together once again in peace and mutual respect."

Mr. Nixon said that he would leave to his prospective Democratic opponents in 1972 "the speculation that you might be a one-term President." His choices for the UN Ambassadorship and the next Secretary of the Treasury should have removed any doubts that he was determined at the close of 1970 to be a two-term President. Congressman and Ambassador-to-be George Bush of Texas, who had lost his race for the Senate, is a rich and bright young Republican who had not previously displayed the "enormous interest in the United Nations" that Mr. Nixon suddenly discovered. The marked differences between Bush, a conservative politician in the best sense of the term, and outgoing White House Counselor Daniel P. Moynihan, Mr. Nixon's first choice for the job, suggested that the President had no clear idea of what the UN required and a very clear idea that potential 1972 vote-winners were required wherever they could be placed.

The votes that Mr. Nixon had immediately in mind were the 26 Texas electoral votes, a fact that became apparent when he appeared in the White House press room on December 14 with his chosen replacement for Treasury Secretary David M. Kennedy. A reporter who telephoned the news to a liberal Democratic senator right after the announcement heard the senator say, *"Connally?*

Not *John* Connally! Not Governor Connally of Texas!" and then break into laughter. It was indeed former Governor John Connally of Texas—a Democrat by formal tie, a profoundly conservative lawyer and rancher and oilmen's man, Lyndon Johnson's man, now become the ideal and superlative Nixocrat. Mr. Nixon, praising Secretary Kennedy while he ousted him and consigned him to the probably empty status and honor of Ambassador-at-Large in the State Department, said that he intended to signify with this appointment that "The problems that we face at home and abroad . . . are not Republican problems or Democratic problems. They are American problems," problems to be approached in the next two years "in a bipartisan spirit." He had tried to recruit at least one prominent Democrat for his first Cabinet and now he had a special kind of Democrat, a politician and official of proven ability but not necessarily one who would achieve the bipartisan miracles the President anticipated. The liberal Democrats and Republicans whom the President professed to be placating in words regarded Connally with more respect than affection and they could be expected to take him for what he clearly was: a stalker for Nixon votes and conceivably, as some people in Washington instantly speculated, Spiro Agnew's replacement on a bipartisan ticket in 1972.

The show of conciliation did not extend to Vietnam. Mr. Nixon indicated, in plain terms that aroused more interpretive argument than they required, that he was prepared to resume the bombing of North Vietnam and inflict upon the whole of Indochina all of the death and destruction that he might deem necessary in order to preserve and continue his policy of phased American withdrawal from South Vietnam. Three times in the course of one answer to a press conference question, he said that he wanted to make clear *"this* President's understanding" of what he was entitled to do if the North Vietnamese so much as dared "by their infiltration" to "threaten our remaining forces" in South Vietnam. In effect, he substituted his "understanding" for Lyndon Johnson's prior "understanding" with Hanoi that in return for a halt to the bombing the North Vietnamese would not bombard South Vietnamese cities, shoot at US reconnaissance planes, or send reinforcements from North to South Vietnam across the demilitarized border zone. He would continue to go through the motions of negotiations in Paris, but "we have no great hopes of them." His statement amounted to a confession, if any were needed, that it was still an open-ended war, to be sustained by indefinite involvement in South Vietnam and expanding involvement in Cambodia.

December 26, 1970

Halfway to Where?

I was still in the stupor induced by the series of press briefings with which the White House celebrated the approaching end of Mr. Nixon's first two years in office, and wondering whether the President and his people could really be suffering from the paranoia that their pleas for understanding and appreciation seemed to suggest, when I came upon a book entitled *The Nixon Poems* (Eve Merriam; Atheneum; $5.95). It is a savage book, illustrated with cruel caricatures in photo montage. Its poems are the kind achieved by printing prose in broken lines and one of them, headed "My Prez," reads in its entirety: *of whom/ else can I say/ that/ when he does/ something good/ there is/ a bad reason for it.*

Reading that squib and others like it, I went a little sick inside. Much that I had written about Richard Nixon in the past two years said or implied the same thing about him. Seeing it in this form and setting, I perceived in it a quality of sour and persistent disbelief that I did not like to recognize but had to recognize in my own work and in my own attitude toward the President. If, in the briefings to which I and other White House reporters had been exposed, the President's assistants and spokesmen had displayed a resentment that was both genuine and disturbing—a feeling that the media and Congress and the public had failed *them,* rather than that they and their President had failed the country—I had to concede upon reflection that there was a basis for their sense of injury. President Nixon had done and tried to do good things for good reasons or, judged at worst, for the mix of "good" and "bad" reasons that is common to us all, and it was true that the good had often been obscured or ignored. Here, I had to admit, was a real problem—for journalists, for Mr. Nixon, for the country.

Departing Counselor Daniel Patrick Moynihan, who was about to leave the White House and return to the Harvard faculty, addressed himself to the problem in one of the year-end briefings. He had been the President's senior in-house Democrat, his most imaginative and innovative assistant, in Mr. Nixon's words his "creative thinker," a certified though somewhat cankered liberal who in his time at the White House had reacted with ever-increasing bitterness to what he considered to be the liberal community's inability and refusal to discern the good in Nixon and in Nixon policies that Pat Moynihan discerned. His farewell discourse was not originally intended for the press, but for the private instruction of the President and his Cabinet and some 200 other officials. It was thought afterward to be so persuasive and penetrating that a few reporters were invited to hear a recording of it, and a transcript was distributed.

Moynihan recalled the fissured country that Mr. Nixon undertook to lead in 1969: "It was coming apart," Moynihan said, what with the divisive agonies of Vietnam, racial and sectional conflict at home, and a corrosive distrust of government that arose from government's failure to deliver what it promised. Remember how it was, consider how it is, and acknowledge—Moynihan pleaded—that receding war, a quieted country, and serious efforts to identify and repair the deficiencies of government comprise "a record of some good fortune and much genuine achievement." And yet, he said in a tone of mourning wonder, "how little the Administration seems to be credited with what it has achieved. To the contrary, it is as if the disquiet and distrust in the nation as a whole has been eased by being focused on the government in Washington."

Why so? In part because (quoting Tocqueville) Americans

relish their anxieties, cherish their cares, and (Moynihan speaking) have "the habit of reducing the most complex issues to the most simplistic moralisms." Excessive moralism "drives out thought," arouses "expectations that cannot be satisfied," and inspires a rhetoric "that constantly, in effect, declares the government in power disqualified for the serious tasks at hand." A current consequence is that "depressing, even frightening things are being said about the Administration. They are not true. This has been a company of honorable and able men, led by a President of singular courage and compassion. . . ."

But not a company of men who were sufficient to the President's need. If the complex problems with which he dealt were to be adequately understood, and his efforts to resolve them were to be adequately appreciated, it would be "necessary for members of the Administration, the men in this room, to be far more attentive to what it is the President has said and proposed. Time and again, the President has said things of startling insight, taken positions of great political courage and intellectual daring, only to be greeted with silence or incomprehension, even in our own ranks. The prime consequence of this is that the people in the nation who take these matters seriously have never been required to take us seriously." Moynihan's serious people (presumably those resistant liberals!) had no interest in assisting a President who did not value them, but the fault was not theirs. The fault lay with Presidential men who failed to follow up their President's pronouncements "with a sustained, reasoned, reliable second and third order of advocacy."

Then followed the most arresting passage in this unusual statement. "Deliberately or no," Moynihan said, "the impression was allowed to arise with respect to the widest range of Presidential initiatives that the President wasn't really behind them. It was a devastating critique. The thrust of the President's program was turned against—him! How else to interpret an attempt to deal with such serious matters in so innovative a way, if in fact the effort was not serious?

"It comes to this. The Presidency requires much of those who will serve it, and first of all it requires comprehension. A large vision of America has been put forth. It can only be furthered by men who will share it." It really comes, of course, to Mr. Nixon. Perhaps, Moynihan said, only those who work with him at the White House can know the President as they know him—"caring, working, hoping for this country that he has made greater already and which he will make greater still."

But—Has he? Will he? The large vision of America that the President has put forth to Pat Moynihan has not been put forth to me. The Nixon vision of America that comes to me is of a country quieted, yes, but in the deadly quiet of protest reduced to futility. The receding war that the Moynihans at the White House see appears to me to be a war that the President promises to end and deliberately prolongs. The President who seemed to me a year ago to have attained a level of decency that I had not thought him capable of attaining presented me and the country with the nomination of Carswell to the Supreme Court—an act of colossal indecency that Mr. Nixon still defends and promises to repeat, given another vacancy, perhaps with a nominee of higher calibre but with the intent of appealing to the same regressive Southerners who hailed Carswell as their champion.

So the problem of belief, the problem that Pat Moynihan addressed and did not resolve, remains for people like me. Mr. Nixon, with his shifts from the stately style and often sound content of his formal messages to his reckless rhetoric on the campaign stump, seems to me to make anything approaching a sustained belief in his wisdom, his compassion, his courage, his good faith impossible. Moynihan blames campaign performances upon "the political process" and the compulsions it places upon politicians: "Elections are rarely our finest hours," he said. "This is when we tend to be most hysterical, most abusive, least thoughtful about problems, and least respectful of complexity." True enough: It was true of Mr. Nixon and of his Vice President, Spiro Agnew, in 1970.

Moynihan quoted the President's remark that "we are in the middle of the journey" and added: "Where it will end, we do not know." I doubt that it will end, for most of the country, in that state of confidence in Richard Nixon that I would prefer to share but cannot share with Professor Moynihan.

January 9, 1971